Slum in a Metropolis

Slum in a Metropolis
The Living Environment

Sudesh Nangia
Sukhadeo Thorat

SHIPRA

ISBN : 81-7541-053-1

First Published in India in 2000

Slum in a Metropolis — The Living Environment

Published by :
SHIPRA PUBLICATIONS
115-A, Vikas Marg, Shakarpur,
Delhi-110092 (India)
Ph : 2458662, 2200954 Fax : 91-11-2458662
Email : siprapub@satyam.net.in

Laser Typeset by :
Sunshine Graphics
Delhi-110032

Printed at :
Chaudhary Offset Process
Delhi-110051

Figure I
Spatial Distribution of Squatters and Resettlement Colonies in Delhi

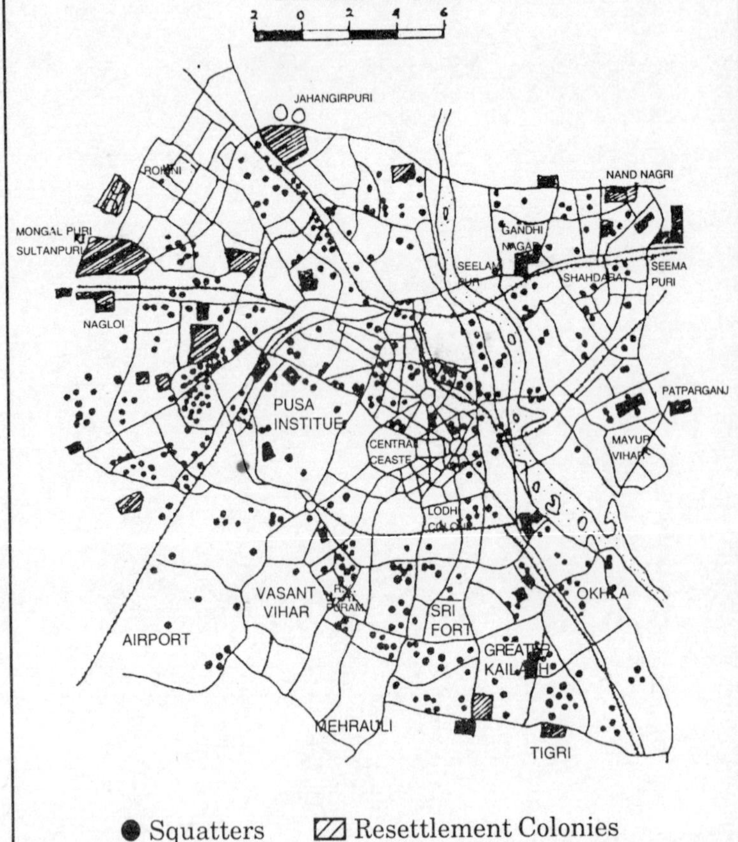

Preface

The right to live in dignity is a basic human right. But visit the slums or the squatter settlements and see for yourself how far this right of humanity is solemnly being persecuted. With more than forty per cent of the population in the metropolitan cities living in slums and squatter settlements and with nearly three-forths of the them living below the poverty line, the right to live with dignity is certainly not being upheld. These people lack the basic facilities of food, shelter, clothing, health, education, etc. They live in a substandard physical environment with poor drinking water, electricity, toilet and sewerage facility. Their housing stock, which consists of semi-permanent building material, can in no way be termed as an asset to be proud of. They may be shunted any time from the place they have built their shelter cn as the land does not being to them. They may be fired from the work without prior notice as they are mostly engaged as casual workers in the informal sector of the urban economy. Their children may roam around the streets, in semi-clad, semi-fed conditions without any future hopes. In this context, there is a need to probe into the living conditions of the people in such settlements and to sensitize the opinion leaders to the need for improvement in the quality of the living environment for the slum and squatter dwellers.

This study, about the living condition of people in a squatter settlement in Delhi, is based on extensive field survey carried out by the M.A. 1st semester students as part of their M.A. programme in Geography, in the Centre for the Study of Regional Development, Jawaharlal Nehru University during 1991–93. The survey was conducted during December 1992. The data collected through the questionnaires were used to examine and analyse the quality of living conditions of the people in a squatter settlement in Kalkaji area of Delhi. The field work was organized by Sudesh Nangia and Sukhadeo K. Thorat, the two faculty members of the centre.

The Department of Special Assistance (DSA), in the Centre for the Study of Regional Development, Jawaharlal Nehru University, provided financial support for processing of the data and computer work. We express our gratitude to DSA for this financial assistance. We also acknowledge the research assistance rendered by Gopa Kumar and Anant Charan Mallick in the culmination of the project. We also thank the residents of the squatter-cluster where field survey was conducted and the eldermen of the settlement who helped us in providing their personal/community-based information in detail.

We tried to collate the information in the best possible manner and present it in the present format. However, lapses may still have crept in on account of partial information/data sets in certain cases which were beyound our control. We hope the readers will bear with the limitations of the text, which otherwise reflects on the demographic and socio-economic profile of the residents, their migration patterns and housing and household amenities.

Centre for Study of Regional Development
School of Social Sciences
Jawaharlal Nehru University
New Delhi

Sudesh Nangia
Sukhadeo Thorat

Contents

List of Tables

CHAPTER 1

Introduction

Urbanization has been taking place at a rapid pace in developing countries, and in India in particular. The urban population increased by almost ten times between 1901 and 1991, and the number of urban settlements doubled during this period to 3,768. The urban population has been steadily increasing over the century, according for about 26 per cent of the population of the country, or 217 million in 1991. The small towns are somewhat stagnating while the metropolitan cities have grown to accommodate about one-third of the total urban population in 1991. The four largest metropolitan cities, Bombay, Calcutta, Delhi and Madras accounted for nearly one-fourth of all urban population.[1] This poly-metropolitan apex of urbanization is due to large-scale migration from poverty-stricken rural areas, besides their own natural increase.

Rapid urbanization, with its employment prospects, attracts a large number of poor people from surrounding regions. Most of them cannot find adequate housing, and squat wherever they find some space, public or private, the proximity of their working areas. This is the beginning of a slum.

The national capital, Delhi, attracts about 70,000 migrants every year. Growth of population has brought about a decline in the quality of living as the slums and squatters have multiplied manifold. The urban infrastructure has become grossly inadequate. It is estimated that seventy per cent of Delhi's population lives in substandard conditions.

Concept and Categories of Slums in Delhi

According to the Slum Areas (Improvement and Clearance)

Act 1956, slums are areas where buildings are (a) in any respect unfit for human habitation; and (b) are by reason of dilapidation, overcrowding, faulty arrangements and design of such building, narrowness or faulty arrangements of streets, lack of ventilation, light or sanitation facilities or any combination of these factors, are detrimental to safety, health and morals.

Delhi has four types of slums, viz. (a) notified slums, (b) unauthorized colonies, (c) resettlement colonies, and (d) squatters (jhuggis).

Notified slums are distributed/defined pockets. The old city of Shahjahanabad (walled city), its extension and certain urban villages have been notified as slums. These slums accommodated around 10 lakh population in 1985.

Unauthorized colonies are areas developed by private colonizers with profitable layout plan without any regard to the need of community facilities as well as the basic amenities required for the individual plot. The number of unauthorized colonies was recorded at 945 till March 1991 and the population living in these areas was estimated to be around 17 lakh as in December 1990.[2]

Resettlement colonies are called so because under the slum clearance programme during 1960–75, the Municipality/Delhi Development Authority has allotted small developed plots and modestly built-up tenements to jhuggi-dwellers in planned and developed colonies. "Under this scheme, 2.14 lakh households were accommodated in these colonies. The community facilities provided to these colonies are found to be non-functional and the living conditions are even poorer than the notified slum areas."[3]

Squatter (jhuggi-jhompri) clusters are spread all over the city. They are a conglomeration of houses built up without regular foundation on public land meant for future development, on drain sides, on the side of railway tracks, on the bank of river Yamuna. These squatter settlements are made of straw, mud, loose bricks, tin, wood corrugated sheets, etc. Without a regular foundation, jhuggis are not arranged in a particular order and haphazard development has taken place. In 1991 it was estimated that jhuggi clusters have accommodated around 12 lakh population in Delhi.[4] Since the squatters are the worst placed among slum-dwellers, our study is based on a squatter settlement in Delhi.

Objective and Study Area

The squatter settlement selected for study is from the South Delhi planning zone as a large number of slums are concentrated in this zone. The squatter settlement, named Bhumiheen Camp, is located near Kalkaji DDA flats, situated five kilometres from Nehru Place in the south-eastern direction, surrounded by the New Okhla Industrial Area, Okhla Industrial Estate and Gobindpuri Extension which has a strong base of industries and factories (Figure I and II).

Main Objective

1. To study the growth and spatial distribution of slums and squatters in Delhi;
2. To evaluate the quality of life in Indian slums taking into account their economic and civice character and living conditions;
3. To understand the demographic characteristics of slum-dwellers;
4. To examine the pattern of migration and to identify the factors behind this process.
5. To analyse the nature of the migration and examine whether there is any shift or change in the migrants' occupation in the process of migration;
6. To study in detail the economic activities i.e., occupational structure, employment, and income status of the squatter dwellers; and
7. To examine the living environment of the squatter settlement.

Data Base and Methodology

Both primary and secondary data have been used. As the census of India does not give the data on slum dwellers separately, the information about all India slum conditions was collected from the National Sample Survey reports in its 31st and 44th rounds carried in the years 1976-77 and 1986-89 respectively. Information about the number and distribution of slums in

Figure II
Location Map of Bhumiheen Camp

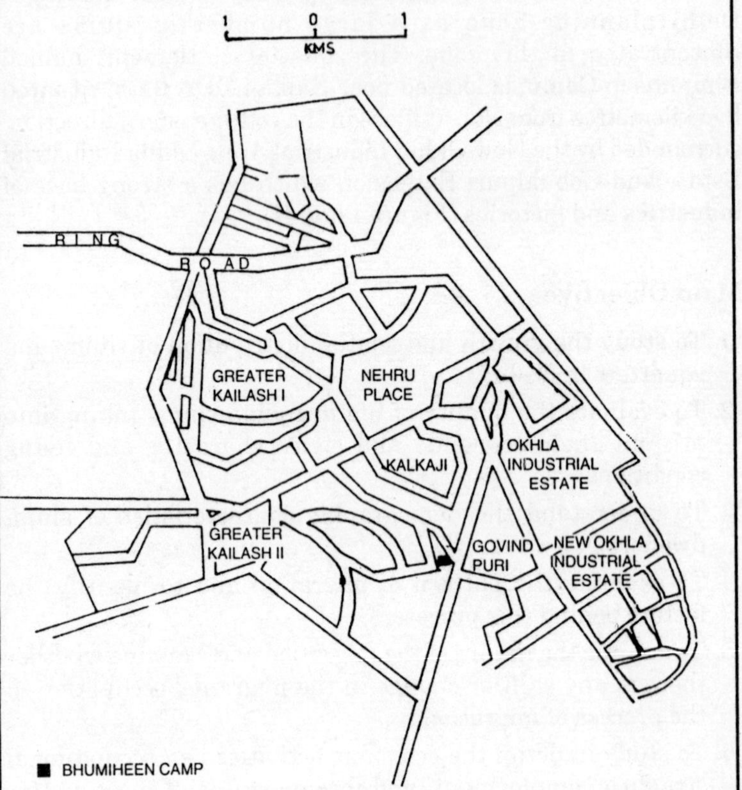

Delhi was collected from the documents of the Slum Wing Development Authority. The data on the squatter settlements have been collected by canvassing questionnaire at household levels. The survey was conducted during December 1991 and January 1992. The household schedule generated the information about the socio-demographic and economic characteristics, migration and infrastructure facilities and civic amenities available to the squatter settlement.

The study is organized into seven chapters, including the introduction and conclusion. The first chapter introduces the parameters of the study and surveys the literature on the subject. In the second chapter, the quality of life in India's slums is discussed, by analysing the socio-economic conditions and facilities available in the slums of class I cities. In the third chapter, the socio-demographic characteristics of the squatter population have been discussed, taking into account age, sex, marital status, educational level, caste, religion and ethnic background. In the fourth chapter, the place of origin of the squatter population, their cause of migration, year of migration, occupation at the place of origin and present occupation, contact in migration have been discussed. The fifth chapter analysed the economic characteristics of the squatter population like work participation rate, industrial classification of workers, employment status, occupation structure, income and distance to work place. The sixth chapter evaluates the living environment of the squatter settlement, by looking into the facilities and amenities available to them. Finally chapter seven summarizes the main findings of the study.

Earlier Literature

The presence of slums and squatter settlements is a clear indication of a society's failure and the failure of government to provide adequate habitat for human development. They are also a constant reminder of the loopholes in urban planning. The term 'slum' is used to indicate housing which falls below a certain level which is necessary to contribute to human development (Aldrich and Sandhu).[5] The term 'squatter settlement' is used to indicate housing that is either the result of illegal occupation or has developed in an unauthorized fashion (World Bank, 1992).[6] United Nations Urban Land policies[7] define slum as a building, group of buildings or areas characterized by overcrowding, deterioration, insanitary conditions or absence of facilities or amenities which because of these conditions or any of them, endanger the health, safety or morals of its inhabitants or the community. A definition which might be of interest is one given by the *Decca Herald,* as a habitat having small tenements, narrow lanes and a lack of sanitation with no thought for the quality of life.[8] Birdi[9] observed that slums are physically areas of the city with inadequate housing, deficient facilities, overcrowding and congestion, and socially, slum is a way of life, having a special character with its own set of norms and values as reflected in poor sanitation, health values, health practices, deviant behaviour and social isolation. The Delhi Development Authority (as defined by Slum Area Improvement and Act, 1956) defines that :

> slums are those areas where the buildings are in any respect unfit for human habitation and are by reason of dilapidation, overcrowding , faulty arrangements of streets, lack of ventilation, light or sanitation facilities or any combination of these factors, are detrimental to safety, health and morals.

A number studies have examined the causes behind the emergence of slums. Rao[10] observed that slums are created mainly because of poverty, social backwardness and unemployment of people living in the countryside, who subsequently move to urban areas as a last resort. The rapid industrialization in the towns and cities provides more opportunities, and thus attracts a large number of people from the surrounding areas. Rao and Rao[11] mentioned three conditions under which slums emerge, namely, squatting of poor migrants; deterioration of group of buildings in the old part of city; and conversion of the villages and peripheral areas into slums due to city expansion.

Hardoy and Satterthwaite, in their study of slum conditions in developing countries (1989)[12] note that slums are developed on most unhealthy and polluted land sites. They also develop in sites subject to high noise levels, close to major highways or airports. The poor groups do not live in these places in ignorance of danger, rather they choose such sites because these sites meet their more immediate and pressing needs. Polluted sites are cheap because they are dangerous and commercially unsuitable. Rao and Rao (1984)[13] observed that slums emerge at the vacant piece of land near the work place.

With few exceptions most studies on slums are based on individual cities. A study of slums in Delhi[14] concluded that the slum areas required prevention of future congestion, planned decentralization of population, economic betterment and clearance programmes. De Souza (1968) analysed the geographic distribution of the poor people who live in slum conditions[15] In Chandigarh, such people were shifted to labour colonies in the fringe sector. Each dweller was allotted on nominal rent a small plot, measuring 9 ft. x 6 ft., but the plots were not evenly distributed among the dwellers. The study points out the limitations of state-sponsored planning towards the rehabilitation of homeless in Chandigarh city. It has provided a shelter to many, but it could not prevent the "structurally located inequality" within the slum dwellers. Only a few of them have taken a lead by constructing attached pucca houses to the original one.

Ghosh and others (1972) have made a detailed survey of Calcutta with special reference to the land-use pattern, the utility services, housing condition and traffic arrangement of the major metropolitan city.[16] They have found that the major concentration of squatter settlements occurs near the railway crossing, local bus depots and in the low-lying areas in the heart of the city. Thus the organic growth of the city is linked with the degeneration of old slum areas and their benefit to the new areas which once again termed to the overall growth of the city. Tanuja (1973) while analysing the morphology of residential areas in Indian cities, has discussed the nature and characteristics of slums.[17] Citing the examples of Kanpur and Delhi, she claims that slum development in India indicates that it is the result of overcrowding and haphazard growth of cities. Immigrants lured by job opportunities in industrial units also take up other occupations, such as petty shopkeeping, domestic servants, milkmen, rickshaw and cart pullers, even beggars. The study, however, did not cover the aspects of market employment-manpower utility syndrome and thereby ends up with a presentation on the facts and related theory. Bose (1973) has made a comprehensive study of the trend of urbanization in India.[18] He has also analysed the nature and spatial characteristics of Indian slums. Sinha (1974) studied the cost aspect of slums in Patna and suggested measures to eradicate this problem from the city.[19] The study however, could not provide a contemporary analysis about the preparedness and the commitment of the executives responsible for the implementation of the development programmes.

Khatu (1975) has examined the nature and characteristics of slums of Baroda and has identified two distinct categories i.e., inherited and satellite slums.[20] The former includes villages which were incorporated into the city during its expansion, while the latter includes the blighted areas that grew around the former on illegally occupied areas. De Souza (1978) has observed that unplanned and haphazard growth of the metropolitan cities in India was a factor for the rapid development of the blighted areas.[21] He estimated that one-fifth of the total urban population (22 million) lived in slums or squatter settlements. In Ahmedabad, nearly 45 per cent of the total urban population lived in slums, and this number is estimated at 2.5 million in Calcutta. He also studied the nature of urban planning, renewal, housing for the poor and socio-economic characteristics of the slums in the background of urban poverty. The studies though provides a rich understanding of the urban problems of India, ignore the extraneous factors like nature of policy, mechanism of market economy and manoeuvring of the industrial class over the very growth of urbanization.

Lahiri (1978) has discussed the urban problems of Calcutta, particularly those arising out of population growth, mass migration, employment situation and transport.[22] He has correlated them with the squatter problem which showed a tendency to grow in the heart of the city. Singh (1979) has made an extensive socio-ecological study of Shillong and its environment.[23] He has studied the land-use pattern and suggested a model pattern for future developments. Sahani (1980) has also discussed the spatial character of the chawls or squatter settlements in Bombay and has stressed the need for public utility service,[24] and their availability to the urban poor.

Rao and Rao (1984) discussed the pattern of growth of slums in Vijayawada and the nature of its social organization.[25] They also discussed the process of migration and the migrants' adjustments to the urban conditions and their occupational mobility in the city economy. Majumdar (1983), in his study of the slums in Delhi,[26] focused to see urbanizing rural migrants in their interactive context of social, economic, cultural and environmental factors. He defined the quality of life in slums in terms of its social and physical dimensions. He also made an attempt to identify the process through which rural migrants overcome their disadvantage, which he thought is a vital element in their development process, through which they became an integral part of the total system of functioning.

Pathak in his study of Calcutta's slums suggested suitable

measures to improve them.[27] Roy (1992) gave a detailed account of the slum situation in Calcutta.[28] Taking into account the sanitation, water and toilet facilities, he mentioned that although some facilities are satisfactory, the problems of garbage disposal, sewerage and waterlogging and flooding are major threats to the environment of the bustee dwellers. Rao (1983)[29] in a study of the slums in Poona focussing on the socio-economic conditions of stone-cutters noted that 74 per cent of the people are below the poverty line. Shafi (1995)[30] remarked that the national capital is becoming the slum capital of India with 929 jhuggi clusters containing a population of 1.7 million which is incidentally more than the city's population in 1947. Discussing the problems in slums, he mentioned that teeming slums lacking safe drinking water, elementary hygiene and! basic sanitation, with putrefying garbage heaps lead to the spread of diseases.

Slums and squatters are components of our urban system and contribute a significant quantity of labour force to the urban labour market and generate adequate income to sustain the urban economy but the slum dwellers are denied the very basic amenities for their sustenance. They live in very squalid conditions. Kundu (1991)[31] in an attempt to examine the magnitude of disparity in the access to basic facilities of the poor people, observed that absence of protected water and sewerage and sanitation facilities in slums creates serious environmental problems to the people. In another study,[32] he argued that the urban poor get only a small share of the basic facilities and have access to only the lower order amenities while the non-poor are getting the larger share of the higher order of services, in per capita terms. According to him, the situation in slums is worse, the water supply in the public stand points is much less than in other areas with low water pressure and short duration of supply. About toilet facility, Kundu (1991, 1994); Majumdar (1983) and Hardoy and Satterthwaite (1989) noted that lack of toilet facility forces people to defecate in open space. Hardoy[33] observed that one-third of the urban people in India have no toilet of any kind while another one-third rely on bucket latrines. One-third may use latrines connected to sewers but only 10 per cent have sewerage connection in their homes. Kundu[34] noted that the conditions of jhuggi-jhompri clusters in Delhi are much worse. Nearly 37 per cent of the households do not have access to any type of latrine or sanitation facilities, 26 per cent use community toilets while only 2.4 per cent have individual toilets. Majumdar[35] found that inadequate facilities for latrine and their over-use by too many persons in the absence of their regular cleaning, had made most of them not only unserviceable but also extremely unhygienic.

Degraded living environment in the slums leads to poor health conditions of their dwellers. The crowed, cramped conditions transmitted diseases like tuberculosis, influenza and meningitis easily. The spread of disease was often aided by low resistance among the malnourished individuals. In Kanpur, one of India's major industrial centres, the development authority estimated that 60 per cent of the children in slums had tuberculosis (CSE).[36] In a study, Basta (1979)[37] observed that in the slums of Delhi, infant mortality rate was 221 per 1000 live births. Among the lowest castes, infant mortality rate was more than double.

In spite of all the problems, their slum people are struggling hard to live and they are trying to create better environment for their descendants so that they may become more dignified members of the society than their predecessors. Sandhu (1985)[38] in his study mentioned that not all slums are areas of darkness and despair. Their poverty may be economic but not socio-cultural.

NOTES

1. K. Sing and F. Steinberg, 1996. In Introduction to *Urban India in Crisis,* K. Sing and F. Steinberg (eds), New Age International Publishers, New Delhi, p. xxix.
2. H.S. Gill, 1992. Housing the Poor—An Analysis with Special Reference to Slum Colonies in Delhi. *Unpublished thesis*, SSS/CSRD, Jawaharlal Nehru University, New Delhi, pp.1–20.
3. Ibid.
4. R.G. Gupta, 1991. "Planning, Development and construction of Urban Spaces in Delhi": An Overview. *Yojana*, 15 April. p.27.
5. B.C Aldrich and R.S. Sandhu (eds), 1995. "The Global Context of *Housing Policy" in Housing the Urban Poor: Policy and Practice in Developing Countries*, Vistar Publications, New Delhi, pp. 17-33.

6. World Bank, *1992. The Housing Indicators Programme*, Washington, DC: The World Bank.
7. K.R. Rao, and M.S.A. Rao, 1964. *Cities and Slums: A Study of Squatters' Settlement in the City of Vijayawada*, concept Publishing Company, New Delhi.
8. *Deccan Herald*, 21st July 1987, Bangalore.
9. H.D. Birdi, 1982. Delhi-Slums and Law: A Comparative Study of Indian and Foreign Law, *ISSD*, Delhi.
10. P.M. Rao, *Environment and Upliftment of Slums in India*, Vohra Publications, Allahabad (U.P.).
11. K.R. Rao, and M.S.A. Rao, op. cit., pp.3–4.
12. J.E. Hardoy and D. Satterthwaite, 1989. *Squatter Citizen: Life in Urban Third World*, Earthscan Publications Ltd., London, p.159.
13. K.R. Rao, and M.S.A. op. cit., p.3.
14. Bharat Sevak Samaj, Slums of Old Delhi: Report of the Socio-Economic Survey of the Slum Dwellers of Old Delhi, Atma Ram and Sons, New Delhi.
15. A. De Souza, "The Challenge of Urban Poverty: An Introduction" in De Souza, A (ed.), *Social Structure of a Planned City*, Orient Longman, New Delhi.
16. M. Ghosh, A.K. Dutta and B. Roy, 1972. *Calcutta: A study in Urban Growth Dynamics*, Calcutta.
17. K.L. Tanuja, "Morphology of Residential Areas in Indian Cities", Singh, R.L. (ed.), op. cit., pp.188–93.
18. A. Bose, 1973. *Studies in India's Urbanization, 1901–1971*, Tata McGraw Hill Publishing Co. Ltd., Bombay.
19. B.N. Sinha, *1974. Past Trends and Present Position of Slum in the Cities of Bihar: With Special Reference to Patna*, Patna Improvement Trust, Patna.
20. B.N. Khatu, 1975. "Baroda Slums: A Case Study in Misuse of Land", *Deccan Geography,* no. 13, pp. 225–34.
21. A. De Souza, 1978. The Challenges of Urban Poverty. An Introduction in *The Indian City: Poverty, Ecology and Urban Development*, De souza, A., Manohar (ed.), Publications.
22. T.B. Lahiri, 1978. "Calcutta—A Million City with a Million Problems" in *Million Cities of India,* Mishra, R.P. (ed.), Vikas Publishing House, New Delhi, pp.48–56.
23. J.P. Singh, 1979. *Urban Land Use Planning in Hill Areas: A Case Study of Shillong*, Inter-India Publications Delhi.
24. R.T. Sahani, 1980. "Slums: The Backlash of Rural Poverty, Bombay's Slum World", *Social Welfare*, vol. XXVII, no. 1-2, pp. 9-11
25. K.R. Rao, and MSA Rao, op. cit.
26. T.K. Majumdar, *1983. Urbanizing Poor: A sociological Study of the Low Income Migrant Community in the Metropolitan City of Delhi*, Lancers Publishers, New Delhi.

27. C.R. Pathak, *1983. Environmental Problems of Calcutta City*, ISEMA Abstract, NATMO, Calcutta.
28. P. Roy and others, 1992. "Measuring bustee environment in Calcutta", *Social Change* 22(1), (March) pp. 120-39.
29. S.N. Rao, 1983. *Social Organization in an Indian Slum: Study of a Caste in Slum*, Mittal Publications, New Delhi.
30. S.S. Shafi, 1995. India's Urban Crisis, *Patriot*, 16 January.
31. A. Kundu, 1991. Micro Environment in Urban Planning: Access of Poor to Water Supply and Sanitation, *Economic and Political Weekly* 26(37), pp. 2167-71.
32. ————, 1989. *In the Name of Urban Poor: Access to Basic Amenities*, Sage Publication, New Delhi.
33. J.E. Hardoy and D. Satterthwaite, 1989. op.cit.
34. A. Kundu, 1991. op. cit.
35. Majumdar, T.K., 1983. op. cit.
36. Centre for Science and Environment, *The State of India's Environment: A Citizen's Report*, Delhi, 1983.
37. S.S. Basta, 1977. Nutrition and Health in Low Income Urban Areas of the Third World, *Ecology, Food and Nutrition* vol. 6, pp. 113-24.
38. R.S. Sandhu, 1985. Slums: Areas of Darkness and Despair? *Eastern Anthropologist* 3(2): (April-June), pp. 151-60.

CHAPTER 2

Slums and Squatter Settlements: Salient Features

Introduction

India's slum population has been growing faster than its urban population. Between 1981 and 1991, the urban population increased from 159.5 million to 218 million, registering an increase of 36.4 per cent. The slum population during this period increased from 27.9 million to 46.3 million, thus registering an increase of nearly 66 per cent during the decade. In 1991, 21.3 per cent of India's urban population lived in slums compared to 1981, when 17.5 per cent of the urban population was slated as slum population. In 1991, among the states, Jammu & Kashmir had the highest percentage of urban population identified as slum population (32.2 per cent). And among the Union territories, Andaman and Nicobar Islands depict maximum of the urban population as slum-dwellers (46.5 per cent). The states of Himachal Pradesh (28 per cent), Maharashtra (25.8 per cent) Meghalaya (25.2 per cent), Sikkim (25.7 per cent), West Bengal (27.8 per cent) and Union Territories of Chandigarh (28.0 per cent), Delhi (26.5 per cent) have a high percentage of their urban population (25–30 per cent) living in slums compared to other states.

Karnataka has the record of the lowest urban population living in slums (9.3 per cent). Other states and Union Territories show varying patterns between the two extremes of Karnataka and Andaman and Nicobar islands.

Though in general, the slum population has indicated a

rise from 1981 to 1991 in most states, some states have also experienced a decline. The states of Mizoram, Nagaland and the Union territories of Andaman and Nicobar Islands, Chandigarh, Dadra and Nagar Haveli, Daman, Diu and Lakshadweep had no slum population in 1981 but added substantially to slum inhabitants by 1991.

The states to experience decline[1] in the percentage of slum population between 1981 and 1991 are Bihar (37.5 to 23.7), Jammu and Kashmir (49.7 to 32.2), Meghalaya (27.4 to 25.2), Punjab (25.1), Delhi (31.2 to 26.5) and Pondicherry (29.8 to 29.6).

The following section gives a profile of various aspects of living environment and the quality of life in slum and squatter settlements in different states of India based upon the data provided by NSS surveys. There is a limited information at the all-India level about slum conditions in various states. The National Sample Surveys provide data for the periods 1976–77 and 1988–89. The discussion is organized into two sections. First, slum conditions in urban India are described on the basis of number of slums, area under slums and estimated slum population in class I cities; socio-economic characteristics of slum population and living environment. In the second section, conditions of slums in Delhi, including their growth of numbers and population are analysed.

Slum Conditions: All India Scenario

Magnitude

The 31st round of NSSO, 1976–77, reported an estimated 18 lakh households and 85.1 lakh people living in 10,200 slums (Table 2.1). The highest percentage of slum population was in Maharashtra (22.65), followed by Tamil Nadu (15.84) and Bihar (14.74). These three states together comprise more than 50 per cent of the slum population of India. In the states of Andhra Pradesh, Delhi and Uttar Pradesh, the slum population varied between 5 and 10 per cent and together, they accommodated 25 per cent of the slum population living in class I cities of India. Gujarat, Madhya Pradesh, Karnataka, Punjab, Rajasthan, Bihar, Kerala and Orissa have 1 to 4 per cent of

TABLE 2.1 : NUMBER OF SLUMS, AREA UNDER SLUMS AND ESTIMATED NUMBER OF HOUSEHOLDS AND PERSONS IN SLUM AREA OF CLASS-I CITIES: 1976–77

State/Union Territory	*Area in acres*	*%*	*Households*	*%*	*Persons*	*%*
All India	75919.57		18099		85112	
Andhra Pradesh	4063.25	5.35	1936	10.70	8948	10.51
Assam	102.31	0.13	15	0.08	54	0.06
Bihar	118659.66	15.62	255	1.41	1271	1.49
Gujarat	1175.28	1.55	614	3.39	3288	3.86
Haryana	146.50	0.19	27	0.15	90	0.11
Jammu & Kashmir	37.00	0.05	25	0.14	145	0.17
Karnataka	4149.32	5.47	578	3.19	3186	3.74
Kerala	966.39	1.27	200	1.11	1221	1.43
Madhya Pradesh	1521.20	2.0	631	3.49	3231	3.80
Maharashtra	23893.90	31.47	3924	21.68	19274	22.65
Meghalaya	76.00	0.10	22	0.12	133	0.16
Orissa	2838.33	3.74	243	1.34	922	1.08
Punjab	833.07	1.10	499	2.76	2382	2.80
Rajasthan	2815.04	3.71	329	1.82	1680	1.97
Tamil Nadu	6691.92	8.81	2760	15.25	13484	15.84
Uttar Pradesh	3638.61	4.79	1067	5.90	5293	6.22
West Bengal	7939.98	10.66	3273	18.08	12551	14.75
Chandigarh	68.00	0.09	56	0.31	223	0.26
Delhi	2970.77	3.91	1610	8.90	7579	8.90
Pondicherry	97.00	0.13	35	0.19	177	0.21

Source: NSS 31st round survey on slum conditions in class I cities 1976-77.

the slum population. The least slum population was reported in six states/Union territories, viz. Chandigarh, Pondicherry, Jammu and Kashmir, Meghalaya, Haryana and Assam (less than 1 per cent). Thus the distribution of slum population shows that three-fourths of the slum population is concentrated in six states and the rest in 14 states.

In terms of slum households, Maharashtra has the largest share (21.7 per cent) followed by West Bengal (18.08 per cent) and Tamil Nadu (15.25 per cent). These three states account for more than 50 per cent of the total slum households in the country. Andhra Pradesh, Delhi and Uttar Pradesh have 5 to 10 per cent of the households registered as slum households and Madhya Pradesh, Gujarat, Karnataka, Punjab, Rajasthan,

Bihar, Orissa and Kerala have 1 to 4 per cent. Chandigarh, Pondicherry, Haryana, Jammu and Kashmir, Meghalaya and Assam registered less than 1 per cent slum households.

Information regarding area under slums shows that, of the total surveyed area of about 75,919 acres of land under the slums, maximum land was in Maharashtra (31.47 per cent) followed by Bihar (15.62 per cent), West Bengal (10.4 per cent) and Tamil Nadu (8.8 per cent). These four states together accounted for almost 80 per cent of the total slum area in class I cities of India. One to six per cent area under slums was reported in ten states/Union territories viz. Karnataka, Andhra Pradesh, Uttar Pradesh, Delhi, Orissa, Rajasthan, Madhya Pradesh, Gujarat, Kerala and Punjab. The remaining six states Haryana, Assam, Pondicherry, Meghalaya, Chandigarh and Jammu and Kashmir reported less than one per cent area under slums.

Socio-economic Characteristics of Slums

The NSSO of 1976–77 provided data on selected socio-economic characteristics of slums in the states (Table 2.2) like household size; number of children in the age-group 0–14 years, population above 15 years (both male and female) per household; sex ratio, percentage of children 5–14 years not attending school; male and female literate; percentage of males and females with job; average monthly per capita expenditure; percentage of households residing in kutcha dwellings and incidence of unemployment.

The household size figures reported largest average size of households in Bihar (6), closely followed by Kerala (5.9). The smallest household size (3.4 people) was reported in the slums of Chandigarh. Rest of the states had an average size between 4 to 5.8 persons per household.

About the number of children 0–14 years per household, maximum number of children was reported in Jammu and Kashmir (2.78), followed by Kerala (2.46), Bihar (2.44), Karnataka (2.4), Gujarat (2.36), Orissa (2.03) and Pondicherry (2.02). Households reporting less than 2 children were in Andhra Pradesh, Maharashtra, Meghalaya, Punjab, Tamil Nadu, Uttar Pradesh, West Bengal, Chandigarh and Delhi.

TABLE 2.2 : SOME SELECTED SOCIO-ECONOMIC CHARACTERISTICS OF SLUM HOUSEHOLDS BY STATES/UNION TERRITORIES 1976-77

State/Union Territory	*Household Size*	*Children per Household*			*Females per 1000*	*Children 5–14 years not attending school (%)*		*Percent Literate*		*Persons with job or at work (%)*		*Average monthly per capita expenditure*	*Household residing in kutcha dwelling units*	*Incidence of unemployment*
		0–14	*F 15+*	*M 15+*		*M*	*F*	*M*	*F*	*M*	*F*			
Andhra Pradesh	4.52	1.02	1.36	1.34	51	54	50	28	55		19	59	62	4.65
Assam	4.03	1.33	1.12	1.58	45	59	69	38	64		77	74	83	2.13
Bihar	6.00	2.44	1.70	1.81	47	73	40	13	52		13	49	31	2.98
Gujarat	5.50	2.36	1.48	1.63	46	55	43	23	50		16	54	37	3.33
Haryana	4.98	2.27	1.31	1.40	45	58	47	12	49		20	50	32	1.31
Jammu & Kashmir	5.55	2.78	1.33	1.44	49	44	40	29	47		8	41	48	-
Karnataka	5.50	2.40	1.54	1.60	48	58	42	24	50		20	48	51	4.11
Kerata	5.90	2.46	1.80	1.64	51	24	72	62	43		22	42	74	12.25
Madhya Pradesh	5.13	2.27	1.40	1.46	48	57	51	22	48		18	53	40	3.12
Maharashtra	4.84	1.96	1.32	1.56	47	40	60	35	52		14	58	28	5.68
Meghalaya	4.68	1.72	1.38	1.58	47	31	68	49	53		13	72	3	-
Orissa	4.76	2.03	1.33	1.40	46	51	44	16	55		15	64	74	-
Punjab	4.53	1.80	1.22	1.50	46	40	53	38	56		10	64	20	-
Rajasthan	5.10	2.30	1.36	1.46	47	60	50	17	47		19	57	31	-
Tamil Nadu	4.57	1.78	1.37	1.40	49	43	57	32	54		22	46	70	9.92
Uttar Pradesh	4.60	1.80	1.23	1.54	45	48	50	28	53		8	54	20	2.93
West Bengal	4.00	1.36	1.01	1.58	42	42	63	41	58		8	69	26	8.65
Chandigarh	3.64	1.41	0.89	1.34	41	45	42	25	72		72	13	71	-
Delhi	4.41	1.72	1.13	1.56	44	43	50	45	57		17	64	19	2.69
Pondicherry	5.17	2.02	1.54	1.61	79	51	46	30	50		14	40	97	-

Source: Socio-economic Conditions of Households in Slums of Class 1 Cities, N.S.S. 31st Round, 1976–77.

The least number of children per household was reported in the slums of Assam (1.33).

The slums of Kerala have maximum number of females of the age of 15 years and above per household (1.8), closely followed by Bihar (1.7). Karnataka and Pondicherry reported 1.54 females per household. The lowest number of females was reported in the slums of Chandigarh (0.89). In the rest of the states/Union territories, only 1 to 1.4 females were reported. As regards number of males 15 years of age and above per household the slums of Bihar had maximum number (1.81), followed by Kerala (1.64), Gujarat (1.63) and Karnataka (1.6). Slums of Chandigarh reported lesser number of both females and males (1.34).

The sex ratio of slum population observed in class I cities was very low even in the states where the state-level sex ratio is very high. Among the states/Union territories, the highest sex ratio was reported in Pondicherry at 79 females per 100 males. It is followed by Andhra Pradesh where the sex ratio is only 51. In the rest of the states/Union territories, the sex ratio was less than 50 females per 100 males. The lowest sex ratio was reported in Chandigarh (41). A very low sex ratio in slums of class I cities is due to male selective migration to the slums.

About male and female literates, the highest level of the male literates was reported in the slums of Kerala (72 per cent) followed by Assam (69 per cent), Meghalaya (68 per cent), West Bengal (63 per cent) and Maharashtra (60 per cent). Fifty to sixty per cent male literacy was reported in Tamil Nadu, Punjab, Delhi, Uttar Pradesh, Rajasthan and Andhra Pradesh. Lowest percentage of literacy among males was reported in Jammu and Kashmir and Bihar (both 40 per cent). In the rest of the states/Union territories, the percentage of male literate was 41–49.

In females literates, states/Union territories showed a very diversified picture. In Kerala the percentage of female literates was 62 and in Haryana only 12. In Meghalaya, the percentage of female literates was reported as 62. After Meghalaya, distant percentage of females literates was reported in Delhi (45) followed by West Bengal (41). Thirty to forty per cent female literates were reported in Punjab, Assam, Maharashtra, Tamil

Nadu and Pondicherry. Less than 30 per cent female literates were found in Jammu and Kashmir, Andhra Pradesh, Uttar Pradesh, Chandigarh, Karnakata, Gujarat and Madhya Pradesh. Lowest figures of female literates were found in Rajasthan (17 per cent), Orissa (16 per cent), Bihar (13 per cent) and Haryana (12 per cent).

There was a high gender disparity in literacy rates in Haryana (0.81), Rajasthan (0.65) and Orissa (0.61). Lower gender disparity was reported in Delhi.

About the children 5–14 years of age not attending school, the highest percentage of children reported in Bihar (73 per cent), followed by Rajasthan (60), Assam (59), Karnataka (58), Haryana (58), Madhya Pradesh (57), Gujarat (55), Andhra Pradesh (54), Pondicherry (51) and Orissa (51). It shows that by and large, education among the slum children is in a highly neglected state. In Kerala, the lowest percentage (24) of children were reported as not attending school.

The information about people with job or at work shows that a highest percentage of males with job or at work was reported in Chandigarh (72), followed by Assam (64), West Bengal (58), Delhi (57), Punjab (56), Orissa (55) and Andhra Pradesh (55). States/Union territories having 50.55 per cent working males were Bihar, Gujarat, Karnataka, Maharashtra, Meghalaya, Tamil Nadu, Uttar Pradesh and Pondicherry. Less than 50 per cent working males were reported in Haryana, Jammu and Kashmir and Rajasthan. In Kerala, a lower level (43 per cent) of males was found with jobs or at work. For females with jobs or at work, figures revealed a vast diversity among various states. Assam reported the highest percentage 77 of females at work, whereas West Bengal, Jammu and Kashmir and Uttar Pradesh reported only 8 per cent females at work. It may be due to higher job opportunities for the females in tea gardens. After Assam, a distant second position of females at work was reported in Kerala and Tamil Nadu where only 22 per cent females were found with jobs.

Gender disparity of the working people shows that maximum disparity was reported in Chandigarh, followed by West Bengal, Uttar Pradesh, Punjab and Jammu and Kashmir. Lower disparity was found in Kerala. Assam shows a negative value due to more female workers than male workers.

The information on average monthly per capita expenditure in slums of class I cities shows that highest monthly per capita expenditure was reported in Assam (Rs 74), followed by Meghalaya (Rs 71) and Chandigarh. Monthly per capital expenditure of Rs 60–70 was reported in West Bengal, Delhi, Punjab and Orissa; Rs 50–60 was reported in Andhra Pradesh, Gujarat, Haryana, Madhya Pradesh, Maharashtra, Rajasthan and Uttar Pradesh; and Rs 40–50 in Bihar, Karnataka, Tamil Nadu and Kerala. The lowest monthly per capita expenditure of Rs 40 was reported in Pondicherry.

Information about instances of unemployment shows that the rate of unemployment is very low in slums. Jammu and Kashmir does not show any unemployment while Kerala shows 12.25 per cent unemployment. As the migration to slums takes place for employment, most of the migrants get absorbed in labour-intensive economic activities in urban centres.

Information regarding households residing in kutcha dwellings shows that higher percentage of households residing in kutcha dwelling was reported in Pondicherry (97 per cent), followed by Assam (74), Orissa (74), Kerala (74), and Tamil Nadu (70). In contrast, Meghalaya has the lowest percentage of kutcha houses (3). Except Meghalaya, Delhi and Uttar Pradesh have 19 per cent and 20 per cent of kutcha houses respectively. Twenty to thirty per cent kutcha dwellings are reported in the slums of West Bengal, Maharashtra; 30–40 per cent in Gujarat, Rajasthan and Haryana and 50–60 per cent in Karnataka. The information indicates that in most of the states/Union territories, most of the slum households are made of kutcha building material.

Number of Households in Slum Areas of Class I Cities by House Ownership

On the basis of ownership, slum-households are divided into three types, viz. owned house, neither rented nor owned house and rented house. The information (Table 2.3) shows that at the all-India level, of the total 18 lakh slum households, only 48.12 per cent are owned, 43.92 per cent are rented and the rest (7.96 per cent) are neither rented nor owned houses. Detailed information on owned houses at state level shows

TABLE 2.3 : ZONE-WISE DISTRIBUTION OF SLUM CLUSTERS AND SLUM SETTLEMENTS IN DELHI

Zone	*No. of Slum Clusters*	*Percentage of Slum Clusters*	*No. of Slum Settlements*	*Percentage of Slum Settlements*
East	212	16.29	123	13.24
Central Zone	139	10.68	93	10.01
North Zone	302	23.21	227	24.40
West Zone	270	20.75	204	22.00
South Zone	378	29.05	282	30.35
Total	1301	100.00	929	100.00

Source: DDA Slum Wing, 1992.

that the highest percentage of owned houses was reported in Jammu and Kashmir (96) and the lowest in Pondicherry (24.14). Twenty to forty per cent owned houses are also reported in Orissa and West Bengal, and 40 to 60 per cent in Assam, Meghalaya, Delhi, Uttar Pradesh, Tamil Nadu, Punjab, Chandigarh, Rajasthan, Karnataka and Andhra Pradesh. 60–70 per cent owned houses were reported in only four states, viz. Gujarat, Kerala, Madhya Pradesh and Maharashtra. Slum households of Haryana reported 88.89 per cent owned houses.

The highest percentage of rented houses was reported in Assam (53.3 per cent) and the lowest in Rajasthan. States reporting up to 10 per cent rented houses are Rajasthan, Chandigarh, Punjab, Jammu and Kashmir and Uttar Pradesh; and 10 to 20 per cent are Haryana, Delhi and Meghalaya; 20 to 30 per cent houses were reported in Kerala, West Bengal, Maharashtra, Bihar, Orissa and Madhya Pradesh and 30 to 40 per cent in Karnataka, Andhra Pradesh and Gujarat. In Pondicherry, 51.22 per cent slum households were rented.

About the category of houses neither rented nor owned, Rajasthan had the highest percentage of such houses (49.14) and Gujarat the lowest (2.7). Slum households of Haryana and Jammu and Kashmir did not have this type of house ownership. A higher percentage of households (40–50) in this category of houses was reported in Meghalaya, Delhi, Uttar Pradesh, Tamil Nadu, Punjab, Chandigarh and Rajasthan.

Latrine facility

At the all-India level, of total households (Table 2.4), only 8.87 per cent households have separate latrine. Of that only 3.59 per cent houses have sanitary types of latrine and the rest (5.28 per cent) are 'other type' latrines. It indicates the severe lapse of the quality of life in the urban slums, even in the class I cities. Detailed information regarding types of latrines (Table 2.4) shows that as for sanitary facility, Delhi has the highest percentage of households having this facility and it is only 7.45 per cent. Punjab reported the lowest percentage of households having this facility (0.17 per cent). In Assam, Haryana, Jammu and Kashmir and Pondicherry, the situation is worse due to lack of separate latrines.

TABLE 2.4 : PERCENTAGE OF HOUSEHOLDS IN SLUMS OF CLASS I CITIES BY SANITARY CONDITION

State / Union Territory	*Separate Latrine*		*No separate latrine*	*Total No. of households*
	Sanitary	*Others*		
All India	3.59	5.28	91.16	18099
Andhra Pradesh	3.87	6.30	89.80	1936
Assam	0.0	26.67	73.33	15
Bihar	3.92	8.24	88.24	255
Gujarat	2.77	5.86	91.53	614
Haryana	0.00	14.81	85.19	27
Jammu and Kashmir	0.00	12.00	88.00	25
Karnataka	4.33	6.06	89.45	578
Kerala	2.50	11.00	86.00	200
Madhya Pradesh	1.58	8.56	89.86	631
Maharashtra	1.58	4.54	93.88	3924
Meghalaya	4.55	22.73	72.73	22
Orissa	6.47	1.29	96.98	232
Punjab	0.71	14.84	72.61	566
Rajasthan	2.41	8.42	45.70	582
Tamil Nadu	7.40	1.63	88.67	2825
Uttar Pradesh	2.48	17.01	71.71	1170
West Bengal	4.23	5.80	89.97	1207
Chandigarh	7.14	0.00	100.00	56
Delhi	9.85	1.56	88.59	1218
Pondicherry	0.00	0.00	100.00	35

Source: N.S.S. 31st Round, 1976–77.

In the category of 'other types' of latrines, Assam has the highest percentage (27) and Delhi has the lowest percentage of latrine of this kind. The Union territories of Pondicherry and Chandigarh found no latrine of this kind.

Except these two sources, no information is available about people having common latrines or not having latrines at all. The instance of defecating in the open are common in India due to lack of latrines even in class I cities. The only information available is "no separate latrine for households". All the households of the Union territory of Pondicherry, a very high percentage of households (90–99) in Orissa, West Bengal, Chandigarh, Maharashtra, Gujarat and Delhi have reported no separate latrine, and a high percentage of households (80–90) in Madhya Pradesh, Andhra Pradesh, Karnataka, Bihar Jammu and Kashmir, Kerala, Haryana and Rajasthan reported no separate latrine. 70–75 per cent slum households of Assam, Meghalaya, Punjab and Uttar Pradesh reported having no separate latrine.

Slum Households by Type and Structure of Buildings

Information available about slum conditions in India for 1988-89, from NSSO, 44th round, is limited to housing only. No information is available on the socio-economic conditions of slums. Due to non-availability of data, a comparison in the slum situation between 1976–77 and 1988–89 to find variation of slum situations over time is not possible. Hence, only those housing conditions of the slums for which data are available in NSS 44th round for the states and Union territories of India and the metropolitan cities are discussed below.

Distribution of Households by Types of Structure of Building

Only 43.4 per cent houses in Indian slums are pucca and another 30.6 per cent are semi-pucca, leaving more than one-fourth houses kutcha (Table 2.5). The housing condition is even worse in some states. In Pondicherry and Manipur, more than 90 per cent structures are kutcha. In Assam, Tamil Nadu,

TABLE 2.5 : PERCENTAGE DISTRIBUTION OF HOUSEHOLDS BY TYPES OF STRUCTURE OF BUILDING IN URBAN SLUMS: 1988–89

States / Union Territory	*Pucca*	*Semi-pucca*	*Kutcha*	*All*
All India	43.39	30.59	26.02	14.68
Andhra Pradesh	34.89	17.11	48.0	18.23
Assam	7.24	26.04	66.64	12.02
Bihar	0.00	0.00	0.00	15.72
Gujarat	43.65	40.42	15.93	10.86
Haryana	52.24	28.57	19.18	4.90
Himachal Pradesh	50.12	35.96	13.69	4.31
Jammu and Kashmir	24.90	56.81	18.29	2.57
Karnataka	27.51	45.93	26.56	16.94
Kerala	46.26	33.64	20.09	4.28
Madhya Pradesh	29.52	49.92	20.51	18.09
Maharashtra	52.08	33.87	14.04	25.42
Manipur	0.00	19.17	80.83	3.13
Meghalaya	24.85	32.60	42.35	5.03
Nagaland	0.00	100.00	0.00	0.44
Orissa	17.20	32.88	49.92	19.07
Punjab	58.12	33.12	8.76	6.28
Rajasthan	59.68	23.70	16.75	8.06
Sikkim	0.00	100.00	0.00	0.63
Tamil Nadu	21.99	19.18	58.83	9.23
Tripura	20.00	53.86	26.14	8.30
Uttar Pradesh	44.91	28.75	26.34	9.53
West Bengal	61.36	25.00	13.64	17.6
Andaman & Nicobar	64.42	16.44	19.14	3.71
Arunachal Pradesh	5.64	22.63	71.72	16.38
Pondicherry	3.02	8.91	88.07	29.17
Bombay	61.39	30.25	8.40	30.61
Madras	24.21	9.16	66.62	15.28
Calcutta	85.17	12.64	2.18	28.87
Delhi	61.57	29.42	9.00	19.44

Source: N.S.S. 44th Round, 1988–89. A Note on Housing Conditions.

Orissa, Andhra Pradesh and Meghalaya, 40 to 70 per cent structures are kutcha. Among metropolitan cities, Madras (Chennai) has 66.63 per cent structures kutcha. In Delhi and Bombay, there is a less percentage of kutcha houses (9 and 8.4 respectively). In Calcutta, kutcha structures are the lowest (2.18 per cent),

Only the slums at Dadra and Nagar Haveli and in Lakshadweep, are all pucca. More than 60 per cent pucca structures are observed in only West Bengal and Andaman and Nicobar Islands and 40 to 60 per cent in Gujarat, Uttar Pradesh, Himachal Pradesh, Maharashtra, Haryana, Punjab and Rajasthan; 20 to 40 per cent in Tripura, Tamil Nadu, Meghalaya, Jammu and Kashmir, Madhya Pradesh and Andhra Pradesh. State/Union territories having only 1 to 10 per cent pucca structures are Pondicherry, Arunachal Pradesh, Goa and Assam.

Of the four metropolitan cities, Calcutta has the highest percentage of pucca structures (88.17), while Madras (Chennai) has the lowest of (24.21) per cent pucca structures. In both Delhi and Bombay (Mumbai), 61.5 per cent households are pucca.

In the slums of Sikkim, Mizoram and Nagaland, all the houses are semi-pucca and in Goa, Jammu and Kashmir and in Tripura, 50 to 70 per cent slums households are semi-pucca. Among the metropolitan cities, Bombay had a maximum 30.25 per cent semi-pucca structure, followed by Delhi (29.4 per cent). In Calcutta and Madras 12.64 per cent and 9.16 per cent of houses were semi-pucca.

Drainage System

Removal and safe disposal of excreta and waste waters coming from washing bathing and other domestic uses is a critical health need. A greater number of the households have no hygienic and adequate means to dispose of waste waters. The information on drainage (Table 2.6) that 44.85 per cent households have no sewerage in the country, and from the rest, 43.62 per cent houses have open and kutcha or pucca type of drainage. Only 11.54 per cent households have underground drainage facilities.

The slums of Nagaland and Pondicherry completely lack sewerage. In most states, half of the slum households have no drainage facility. About one-fifth (20.5 per cent) of slum households have drainage facilities in Gujarat, Punjab, West Bengal, Rajasthan, Maharashtra, Haryana, Uttar Pradesh, Manipur, Himachal Pradesh and Meghalaya. Among the

TABLE 2.6 : PERCENTAGE DISTRIBUTION OF HOUSEHOLD BY DRAINAGE PATTERN

State / Union Territory	*No drainage*	*Open pucca and kutcha*	*Under-ground*	*All*
All India	44.85	43.62	11.54	14.65
Andhra Pradesh	52.85	29.31	17.84	18.22
Assam	78.79	21.21	0.0	12.02
Bihar	48.82	46.03	5.15	15.73
Gujarat	44.84	20.81	34.35	10.86
Haryana	31.90	68.10	0.00	4.89
Himachal Pradesh	24.36	61.48	14.15	4.31
Jaminu and Kashmir	60.74	39.26	0.00	2.42
Karnataka	53.38	39.25	7.37	16.28
Kerala	84.11	11.45	4.44	4.28
Madhya Pradesh	49.03	42.07	8.90	18.09
Maharashtra	33.79	55.55	10.66	25.42
Manipur	29.71	70.29	0.00	3.13
Meghalaya	20.52	79.48	0.00	5.02
Nagaland	100.00	0.00	0.00	0.44
Orissa	85.91	12.27	1.81	18.74
Punjab	43.63	49.20	7.17	6.28
Rajasthan	36.60	60.42	2.98	8.06
Sikkim	0.00	100.00	0.00	0.63
Tamil Nadu	74.46	19.16	6.39	9.24
Tripura	76.14	23.86	0.00	8.30
Uttar Pradesh	31.44	61.20	7.36	9.51
West Bengal	39.05	44.07	16.88	17.54
Pondicherry	100.00	0.00	0.00	28.02
Bombay	11.07	76.38	12.54	30.61
Madras	79.71	9.36	10.93	15.28
Calcutta	17.25	45.23	37.53	28.70
Delhi	22.99	58.95	18.06	19.44

Source: N.S.S. 44th Round, 1988–89. A Note on Housing Conditions.

metropolitan cities, the proportion of slum households without drainage system is 80 per cent for Madras (Chennai), 23 per cent for Delhi, 17.25 per cent for Calcutta and 11.7 per cent for Bombay (Mumbai).

Most states have less than 50 per cent of slum households with open kutcha and pucca type of drainage. States having

50 to 70 per cent sewerage are Maharashtra, Rajasthan, Uttar Pradesh, Himachal Pradesh and Haryana. In Manipur, 70 per cent and in Meghalaya, 79.5 per cent slum households have this type of drainage. Among the metropolitan cities, the slums of Bombay have 76.3 per cent followed by Delhi with 59 per cent and Calcutta with 45.23 per cent households with open and pucca type of drainage. In Madras, only 9.36 per cent households have this type of drainage.

Most households in a large number of states have no underground drainage. The states/Union territories of Nagaland, Pondicherry, Assam, Haryana, Jammu and Kashmir, Manipur and Meghalaya show no underground drainage, while only up to 10 per cent of the slum households have access to it in Orissa, Rajasthan, Kerala, Bihar, Tamil Nadu, Punjab, Uttar Pradesh, Karnataka and Madhya Pradesh. In Maharashtra, Himachal Pradesh, West Bengal and Andhra Pradesh 10 to 20 per cent slum households have this facility. In Gujarat, a higher percentage (34.3) of slum households have this type of facility. Among the metropolitan cities, Calcutta has 37.5 per cent, Delhi 18.6 per cent, Bombay 12.54 per cent and Madras only 11 per cent of the slum households with underground sewerage.

Risk of Water-logging and Flooding

Slums are generally located on grounds with no infrastructure where the chance of eviction is less and where land is unsuitable for commercial development. Slums also develop on river banks, drain sites, flood plains, and in lower parts of the cities, where the risk of water-logging and flooding creates a major problem, and takes a serious toll on health. At the all-India level, more than one-fourth of the slum households face problems of waterlogging and water entering the premises in the monsoon and 2.16 per cent households face the danger of flooding from sea and river (Table 2.7). State-wise information shows that the highest level of 61.06 per cent households in Madras (Chennai) face waterlogging and water entering into the premises in the monsoon, followed by Delhi (44.3 per cent) and Manipur (44 per cent). Between 30 and 40 per cent households face this problem in the slums of Haryana, Calcutta,

TABLE 2.7 : PERCENTAGE DISTRIBUTION OF HOUSEHOLDS BY FLOOD RISK OF BUILDINGS AND LOCATION IN SLUM BUSTEE

States/Union territories in monsoo	*No flood risk*	*Water logging*	*Flood risk from sea/river etc.*	*All*
All India	69.55	28.29	2.16	14.68
Andhra Pradesh	71.71	24.88	3.41	18.17
Assam	76.96	8.24	14.81	12.02
Bihar	78.96	15.64	5.40	15.73
Gujarat	66.30	20.72	12.98	10.86
Haryana	33.06	40.61	26.33	4.90
Himachal Pradesh	100.00	0.00	0.00	4.31
Jammu and Kashmir	80.93	19.07	0.00	2.57
Karnataka	75.03	24.97	0.00	16.94
Kerala	54.67	26.17	19.16	4.28
Madhya Pradesh	84.82	13.62	1.56	17.99
Maharashtra	70.97	27.07	1.97	25.42
Manipur	55.91	44.09	0.00	3.13
Meghalaya	92.23	7.77	0.00	5.02
Nagaland	100.00	0.00	0.00	0.44
Orissa	87.68	11.22	1.10	19.08
Punjab	46.90	38.58	14.51	5.65
Rajasthan	90.71	8.67	0.62	8.07
Sikkim	100.00	0.00	0.00	0.63
Tamil Nadu	58.32	29.81	11.88	9.26
Tripura	88.31	11.69	0.00	8.30
Uttar Pradesh	65.16	30.95	3.88	9.53
West Bengal	63.52	35.17	1.31	17.60
Andaman & Nicobar	64.15	35.85	0.00	3.71
Arunachal Pradesh	73.79	26.21	0.00	16.48
Dadar & Nager	100.00	0.00	0.00	11.16
Goa	65.96	34.04	0.00	7.11
Lakshdweep	100.00	0.00	0.00	1.08
Mizoram	100.00	0.00	0.00	2.75
Pondicherry	65.93	34.07	0.00	29.15
Bombay	60.47	37.80	1.73	30.61
Madras	23.69	61.06	15.25	15.28
Calcutta	60.89	39.11	0.00	28.87
Delhi	49.07	44.29	6.64	19.44

Source: N.S.S. 44th Round, 1988–89. A Note on Housing Conditions.

Punjab, Bombay, Andaman and Nicobar Islands, West Bengal, Goa and Uttar Pradesh and 20 to 30 per cent in Tamil Nadu, Maharashtra, Arunachal Pradesh, Kerala, Karnataka, Andhra Pradesh and Gujarat, and 5 to 10 per cent in Bihar, Madhya Pradesh, Tripura, Orissa, Rajasthan, Assam and Meghalaya. Only the slums of Nagaland, Sikkim, Dadra and Nagar Haveli and Lakshadweep do not face this problem.

The risk of flooding from river/sea in maximum in Haryana (26.3 per cent) followed by Kerala (19.6 per cent) and Madras (15.26 per cent). 10 to 15 per cent slum households facing this problem from the river or sea are in Assam, Punjab, Gujarat and Tamil Nadu. Other states have either low or no risk.

Slums and Squatter Settlements in Delhi

The slum and squatter population of Delhi was estimated to be around 2.3 lakh in 1990. In fact, in 1951, there were only 12,749 persons living in squatter settlements. The number of squatter settlers and the number of people living in them increased considerably by 1975 (see Table 2.8) and then in 1976–77, during the emergency, the squatter settlers were located in resettlement colonies. The fresh stock of poor rural migrants kept moving into the city unchecked and from 20,000 slum and squatter dwellers the figure shot up to 2,30,000 in 1990 as revealed from the following tables.

In 1951, there were only 12,749 jhuggis (squatter settlements) in Delhi. In subsequent years, the number increased very fast (twenty times) and reached 2.5 lakh jhuggies in 1991. These 2.5 lakh jhuggies are unevenly distributed over Delhi in 1301 juggi clusters (squatter-settlement cluster). In Delhi, south zone has the largest number of jhuggi clusters (29.05 per cent), followed by north zone (23.21 per cent) and west zone (20.75 per cent) (Table 2.9).

All the 1301 slum clusters are grouped into 929 slum and squatter settlements. The zone-wise distribution of slums and squatters shows that again the south zone has the highest share of settlements (30.3 per cent), followed by north zone (24.4 per cent) and west zone (22 per cent). In the east zone and in central zone, the lowest percentage of slums and squatters are located (13.24 and 10 per cent respectively). The

TABLE 2.8 : DELHI — GROWTH OF SQUATTER SETTLEMENTS

Year	*No. of Squatter Families*
1951	12,749
1956	22,415
1958	40,000
1961	42,815
1962	66,000
1966	42,668
1971	62,594
1973	98,438
1975	1,50,000
1976-77	20,000
1980	98,709
1981-83	1,13,386
1987	2,00,000
1990	2,30,000

Source: B. Mishra, R.B. Singh, Anupma Malik, "Delhi Metropolis: Housing and Quality of Life". Chapter II, pp. 1962–28 In Million Cities of India Vol. I edited by R.P. Misra, Kamlesh Missra 1998, p. 425.

TABLE 2.9 : GROWTH OF SLUMS IN DELHI

Year	*No. of slum households*	*Percentage change*
1951	12749	-
1956	22415	76
1961	42815	91
1966	42668	-0
1971	62594	47
1973	98438	57
1977	20000*	-392
1981	98709	394
1983	129000	31
1985	150000	16
1987	171000	14
1988	210000	23
1991	259344	23

Note: The decrease is due to large-scale slum clearance.

Source: N. Sridharan, 'Indian slums: Problems, Policies and Issues', in B.C. Aldrich and R.S. Sandhu (eds), *Housing the Urban Poor: Policy and Practice in Developing Countries,* Vistaar Publications, New Delhi, p. 389.

availability of large open spaces, employment opportunities in industries and post-independence colonies and construction sites, resulted in the mushrooming of slum and squatter settlements in south Delhi area. (Table 2.10)

TABLE 2.10 : ZONE-WISE DISTRIBUTION OF SLUM CLUSTERS AND SLUM SETTLEMENTS IN DELHI

Zone settlements	*No. of slum clusters*	*Percentage of slum clusters*	*No. of slum settlements*	*Percentage of slum*
East zone	212	16.29	123	13.24
Central zone	139	10.68	93	10.01
North zone	302	23.21	227	24.40
West zone	270	20.75	204	22.00
South zone	378	29.05	282	30.35
	1301	100	929	100

Source: DDA slum Wing, 1992.

In the classification of slum settlements in terms of number of households a large number of settlements have less number of households and few settlements have a high concentration of households. Only 29 settlements have more than 1500 households each while 259 settlements have less than 50 households each. (Table 2.11)

TABLE 2.11 : DISTRIBUTION OF SLUM SETTLEMENTS INTO VARIOUS SIZES

Settlement size	*No. of settlements*	*Percentage*
Less than 50 jhuggies	359	30.64
51--100 jhuggies	150	16.14
101–300 jhuggies	226	24.30
301–500 jhuggies	78	8.39
501–1000 jhuggies	58	6.24
1001–1500 jhuggies	29	3.12
More than 1500 jhuggies	29	3.12
	929	100.00

Source : DDA Slum Wing, 1992.

Slum and Squatter Population

There is no information about the exact figure of the slum population except some estimations. The first estimation of slum population was done by NSSO, 31st round[2] in the year 1976–77. Accordingly, there was 6.4 lakh slum population in Delhi which accounted for about 23 per cent of the total population of Delhi. In the year 1981, Delhi Development Authority[3] estimated 53 per cent of Delhi's population as slum dwellers, which includes 4.09 lakh squatter population and 9.02 lakh people in unauthorized colonies. The latest estimation was given by R.G. Gupta[4] in 1991. According to him, 64 lakh people were living in substandard areas of Delhi, which accounted for 76.42 per cent of the total population of Delhi. These 64 lakh people were divided into 12 lakh people in jhuggi clusters, 8 lakh in slum-designated areas, 12 lakh in resettlement colonies, 6 lakh in urban villages, 12 lakh in Authorized/regularized colonies and the rest 5 lakh in unauthorized colonies.

The main cause of this alarming growth of slum and squatter population in Delhi is large-scale immigration. According to H.D. Shourie,[5] every year there is an addition of 70,000 migrants to Delhi. In the past three decades, half of the increase in population has been due to migration, the other half being due to urban growth.

The squatter population of Delhi was estimated to be around 2–3 lakh in 1990. In fact, in 1951, there were only 12,749 persons living in squatter settlements. The number of squatter settlements and the number of people living in them increased considerably by 1975 (as the table reveals), and then in 1976–77, during the Emergency the number reduced to only 20,000 because of resettlement of squatter dwellers in resettlement colonies specially designed for them. The fresh stock of poor rural migrants kept moving into the city unchecked and from 20,000 squatter dwellers in 1976–77, the figures shot up to 2,30,009 in 1990.

Conclusion

The quality of life in Indian slums and squatter settlements is poor. People live in subhuman conditions due to lack of basic amenities. Although most of the people are employed, their wages are not enough to meet the daily expenses. They cannot afford a conventional pucca house and a serviced site. Above all, there is no provision for safe disposal of households waste. In most of the slums (44.8 per cent), there are no hygienic and adequate means of disposal of waste waters. Whenever they exist, it is mostly in the form of open drainage.

There is also a threat of water-logging and flooding and water entering into premises during monsoon months and flooding from the rivers as slums normally come up on rivers banks, flood plains, drain sites, etc. Socially and economically, slum dwellers are poor. Illiteracy is the main feature in the slums. Demographically, the slums are unbalanced due to age-sex selective migration specially of the rural poor to the urban area. There is also a high proportion of population of young adults (15–35 years) in the productive age group.

NOTES

1. Central Statistical Organization, Compendium of Environment Statistics, 1997, pp. 162.
2. Conditions of slums in cities, NSSO 31st Round, July 1970–July 1977, vol. III no. 4, pp. 187–90.
3. H.S. Gill, 1983. *Housing the Poor: An Analysis with Special Reference to Slum Colonies in Delhi*, unpublished Ph.D. thesis, JNU, New Delhi.
4. R.G. Gupta, 1991. Planning, Development and Construction of Urban Spaces in Delhi: An Overview, *Yojna*, 15 April, New Delhi, 1991, pp. 26–27.
5. H.D. Shourie, 1998. Frightening Facts on Housing, *The Statesman*, New Delhi, 10 January 1988.

CHAPTER 3

Social and Demographic Profile

In this chapter we analyse the demographic characteristics of the squatter settlements with particular reference to the size, age, sex, marital status and educational level of the sample population in the squatter settlement. Earlier studies have generally shown that slum areas are characterized by high density, low sex ratio, high dependency ratio and less educated people. A detailed analysis with respect to these aspects is undertaken in the following section.

Religion and Caste Composition

Tables 3.1 and 3.2 give details of the squatter population by religion and caste. Of the total population, almost 88.45 per cent are Hindus and 10.21 per cent are Muslims. Other religious groups are negligible at less than one per cent each.

TABLE 3.1 : POPULATION BY RELIGIOUS GROUPS

Religion	*Population*	*Percentage share*
Hindu	4988	88.45
Muslim	576	10.21
Christian	14	0.24
Sikh	43	0.76
Buddhists and others	18	1.32
Total	5639	100.00

Scheduled castes account for nearly 55.70 per cent population followed by 22.12 per cent other backward classes (22.12 per cent) and 20.58 per cent higher caste people. The scheduled tribes account for only 1.58 per cent of the squatter population.

TABLE 3.2 : POPULATION BY CASTE GROUP

Caste	*Population*	*Percentage share*
Scheduled Caste	2787	55.70
Scheduled Tribe	79	1.58
OBCs	1107	22.12
Higher Caste	1030	20.58
Total	5639	100.00

Note: OBCs = Other Backward Classes.

The language spoken by the people is taken as an indicator of their ethnicity. Indirectly this also reveals their background in terms of their state of origin. More than 15 languages and dialects are spoken by the squatter dwellers. Some languages are spoken by a large number of people while most of the languages are spoken by fewer number of people. It is seen from Table 3.3 that 48.02 per cent people speak Hindi and 37.01 per cent people speak Bengali, according for 85 per cent of the slum population. Bhojpuri is spoken by 5.26 per cent people, followed by Urdu (3.35 per cent), Maithili (2.34 per cent) and Parsee (1.34 per cent). Languages or dialects like Punjabi, Rajasthani, Haryanvi, Gujarati, Oriya and Sindhi are spoken by less than one per cent each.

TABLE 3.3 : LANGUAGE BACKGROUND OF SQUATTERS

Language / dialect	*Number of people*	*Percentage*
Hindi	2708	48.02
Bengali	2087	37.01
Bhojpuri	297	5.26
Urdu	189	3.35
Maithali	132	2.34
Parsie	76	1.34
Punjabi	45	0.80
Rajasthani	33	0.58
Haryanavi	24	0.42
Gujarati	13	0.23
Oriya	13	0.23
Sindhi	6	0.10
Other languages	12	0.21
Total	5635	100.00

Sex and Age Composition

The total squatter population is 5639, 54.23 per cent of them males. The sex ratio is 850 females per 1000 males. A lower sex ratio for a squatter population is not uncommon, due to male-selective migration.

The male-female composition of the population, both by religion and caste is given in Table 3.4. The table shows that except Christians (with a sex ratio of 1000 females per males) and Buddhists (with a sex ratio of 1250), all other religions have a lower sex ratio. The Scheduled Caste population has a sex ratio of 882, followed by higher castes (872) and other backward classes (729).

TABLE 3.4 : SEX RATIO BY RELIGION AND CASTE

Caste	*Persons*	*Male*	*Female*	*Sex ratio*
Total population	5639	3047	2592	850
Hindu	4988	2710	2278	840
Muslim	576	279	279	939
Christian	14	7	7	1000
Sikh	43	25	10	720
Buddhist and other religions	18	8	10	1250
Scheduled Caste	2787	1481	1306	882
Scheduled Tribe	79	45	34	755
Higher Caste	1030	550	480	872
OBCs	1107	640	467	729

Age Composition

The age-wise composition of the sample population is presented in Table 3.5. In order to know the number of infants, young and old people and the dependency ratio, the formation of the age groups is arranged accordingly and not by regular five-yearly intervals.

The age data of the squatters shows that more than 40 per cent of the people are below 15 years of age and 3.60 per cent are of the age of sixty and above. About 75 per cent are in the age group of 50–59 years.

Among the young, 5.34 per cent are infants, 10.53 per cent

TABLE 3.5 : PERCENTAGE DISTRIBUTION OF POPULATION BY AGE GROUPS

Age groups	*Population*	*Percentage*	*Cumulative percentage*
0-1	301	5.34	5.34
1-4	594	10.53	15.87
5-9	975	17.29	33.16
10-14	653	11.58	44.74
15-24	895	15.90	60.64
25-34	1084	19.22	79.86
35-59	933	16.54	96.40
60+	204	3.60	100.00
Total	5639	100	—

are 1–4 years of age, 17.29 per cent 5–9 years and rest 11.58 per cent are 10–14 years. Among the middle-aged, most are in the age group 25–34, followed by people aged 35–39 years and 15–24 years of age.

Age composition by sex is given in Table 3.6 and Fig. 2.1. It indicates that, after the age of 10 years, there is a sudden decrease of the young people up to age of 15 years and among them the decrease in girls is more than the boys. This decrease in young boys and girls may be due to a number of reasons such as death, outmigration of boys from slums, outmigration of girls to their native place, marriage or marriageable age, etc. After the age of 15 there is an increase in population up to the age of 25 years. In this group the inclusion of girls is more than the boys. The inclusion of boys may be due to migration for employment and girls due to marriage. As we know, in slums male-selective migration is more prominent. The married menfolk bring their wives after they settle themselves. This phenomenon emerges even more clearly in the age group 25–34. In this group in fact the females are more than the males. In the age group 35–39, the population decreased, and the decrease is entirely due to females as the number of the males shows an increase. The increase in the number of males may be due to availability of work. In case of females it is different, they are not absorbed in the job market at that age. Secondly, the high age of females push them to stay at home or to go back to their native place leaving their menfolk behind.

TABLE 3.6 : PERCENTAGE DISTRIBUTION OF POPULATION OF EACH SEX BY BROAD AGE GROUPS

Age group	*Total*	*M*	*M %**	*F*	*F %**	*% of population#*	
						M	*F*
0-1	301	166	5.45	135	5.21	55.15	44.85
1-4	594	320	10.51	274	10.57	53.87	46.13
5-9	975	517	16.98	458	17.67	53.02	46.98
10-14	653	370	12.15	283	10.92	56.67	43.33
15-24	895	449	14.74	446	17.20	50.17	49.83
25-34	1084	531	17.44	553	21.33	49.00	51.00
35-59	933	598	19.64	335	12.92	64.10	35.90
60+	204	96	3.15	108	4.16	47.06	52.94
Total	5639	3045	100.00	2592	100.00	54.00	46.00

Note: * showing percentage on vertical total; # showing percentage on horizontal total.
M = male; F = female.

After the age of sixty, the population is reduced drastically. This large-scale decrease may be due to death or due to migration from slums to native place. In this age group, the females are more than the males.

Marital Status

The distribution of the squatter people by marital status is given in Table 3.7. The marital status is categorized into five categories, viz. (a) unmarried, (b) married, (c) widowed,

TABLE 3.7 : DISTRIBUTION OF POPULATION BY MARITAL STATUS

Marital status	*Total*	*% of Pop.*	*M*	*F*	*% M*	*% F*
Unmarried	2984	52.92	1727	1257	57.87	42.13
Married	2483	44.03	1285	1198	51.75	48.25
Widowed	160	2.84	27	133	16.87	83.13
Divorced	6	0.14	4	2	66.67	33.33
Separated	6	0.07	3	3	50.00	50.00
Total	5639	100.00	3047	2592		

Note: M = male; F = female.

(d) divorced and (e) separated. It is observed from the table that the unmarried outnumber the married. Unmarried males are more than unmarried females. This may be due to two reasons: male-selective migration to the slums and higher age at marriage of males than the females (Premi and others 1983).[2] Among the married, the males are more than the females. This may also be due to male-selective migration.

Among the widowed, females outnumber males, in the ratio of 83.13 : 16.87. As we have seen, females outnumber males at old age, and the death of males in old age increases the number of widows. Among the divorced and separated, males slightly outnumber the females.

Table 3.8 presents the marital status by religion and caste. Among the Buddhists and other religions, and among Scheduled Tribes, the married outnumber the unmarried, may be due to early age at marriage among these groups.

Widowhood is more among Hindus, Buddhists and other religious groups and among Scheduled Tribe and Scheduled Caste people. No widowed are found among Christians. While more separated people are found among Muslims and higher caste people; no separated people are there among the Christians, Sikhs, Buddhists and other religious people and among Scheduled Castes and Scheduled Tribes.

Literacy and Educational Level

Table 3.9 shows the educational level of the squatter people. It is seen that about 40 per cent of the people are illiterate. Among the literates, around 27 per cent are educated up to primary school, 17.80 per cent up to middle school, 11.19 per cent up to matric level, 1.36 per cent up to 12th class and only 0.42 per cent up to graduation. Thus the major concentration of literates is in the primary and middle level.

Gender differences in literacy rate and educational level are quite evident. The females are less educated than the males. While the literacy rate among the male is 77 per cent, it is only 47 per cent among the females. The table shows that there is no significant difference between males and females in the ratio at primary level, but the disparities emerge prominently after middle school. The ratio for female is lower

TABLE 3.8 : MARTIAL STATUS BY RELIGION AND CASTE GROUP

Religion / caste	*Un-married*	*Married*	*Widowed*	*Divor-ced*	*Separa-ted*	*Total*
Population	2984	2483	160	6	6	5639
	(52.92)	(44.03)	(2.84)	(0.10)	(0.10)	(100)
Hindu	2632	2195	150	6	5	4988
	(52.76)	(44.00)	(3.00)	(0.12)	(0.10)	(100)
Muslim	314	253	8	-	1	576
	(54.51)	(43.92)	(1.34)	-	(0.17)	(100)
Christian	8	6	0	-	-	14
	(57.14)	(42.86)	-	-	-	(100)
Sikh	23	19	1	-	-	43
	(53.49)	(44.18)	(2.32)	-	-	(100)
Buddhists and others	7	10	1	-	-	18
	(38.89)	(55.55)	(5.55)	-	-	(100)
Scheduled caste	1477	1213	94	3	2	2787
	(53.00)	(43.52)	(3.37)	(0.10)	(0.7)	(100)
Scheduled tribe	37	39	3	-	-	79
	(46.83)	(49.37)	(3.80)	-	-	(100)
Higher caste	549	452	24	2	3	1030
	(53.30)	(43.88)	(2.33)	(0.19)	(0.29)	(100)
OBCs	577	500	29	1	-	1107
	(52.12)	(45.16)	(2.61)	(0.09)	-	(100)

Note: Figure in the bracket refer to percentage share in total.
OBCs = Other Backward Classes.

TABLE 3.9 : LITERACY AND EDUCATION LEVELS

Educational level	*Total*	*% of Total*	*M*	*% M*	*F*	*% F*
Illiterate	2380	42.20	995	32.65	1385	53.43
Primary	1523	27.00	789	25.89	734	28.32
Middle	1004	17.80	665	21.82	339	13.08
High Sec.	631	11.19	510	16.74	121	4.67
Inter	77	1.36	66	2.16	11	0.42
Degree	24	0.42	22	0.72	2	0.08
	5639	100.00	3047	100.00	2592	100.00

Note: M = male; F = female.

than that of male at middle, higher secondary, intermediate and college level.

Literacy rate as well as educational levels very across religion and caste groups. Table 3.10 shows that literacy rate is lower among Muslims, Hindus and Christians as compared to Buddhists, Sikhs and other religious groups. Literacy is lowest among the Muslims. Among caste groups literacy rate is the lowest among the Schedule Castes followed by Other Backward Classes and Schedule Castes. It is the highest among the high castes. In educational level, the ratio of those educated to the primary level is highest among the Hindus, followed by Muslims, Christians, Sikhs and others. Among caste groups, Other Backward Classes (OBCs) show a higher ratio in primary level as compared to other groups. It is the lowest for Schedule Tribes.

TABLE 3.10 : RELIGION AND CASTE BASED DISTRIBUTION OF POPULATION BY EDUCATIONAL LEVEL

	Illit-erate	*Prim-ary*	*Middle*	*Higher Second.*	*10+2*	*Degree*	*Total*
Total population	2380	1523	1004	631	77	24	5639
	(42.00)	(27.00)	(17.80)	(11.19)	(1.36)	(0.42)	(100)
Hindu	2093	1373	866	565	68	23	4986
	(41.98)	(27.54)	(17.37)	(11.33)	(1.36)	(0.46)	(100)
Muslim	260	138	117	52	8	1	576
	(45.14)	(23.96)	(20.31)	(9.03)	(1.39)	(0.17)	(100)
Christian	7	2	5	-	-	-	14
	(50.00)	(14.29)	(35.71)	-	-	-	(100)
Sikh	15	8	11	9	-	-	43
	(34.88)	(18.60)	(25.58)	(20.93)	-	-	(100)
Buddhists and others	5	2	5	5	1	-	18
	(27.80)	(11.10)	(27.80)	(27.80)	(5.50)	-	(100)
Scheduled castes	1228	715	485	308	35	14	2787
	(44.06)	(25.65)	(17.40)	(11.05)	(1.25)	(0.50)	(100)
Scheduled tribes	36	14	17	6	6	0	79
	(45.47)	(17.72)	(21.52)	(7.60)	(7.60)	-	(100)
Higher castes	365	299	212	132	17	5	1030
	(35.43)	(20.03)	(20.59)	(12.81)	(1.65)	(0.48)	(100)
OBCs	475	345	155	118	11	3	1107
	(42.90)	(31.16)	(14.16)	(10.67)	(1,00)	(0.27)	(100)

Note: Figures in brackets show percentage share in total population.

Educational level up to matriculation by religious groups shows that the ratio is higher among the Christians, Muslims, Sikhs and Buddhists but relatively lower among Muslims and Hindus. Similarly the Sikhs and Buddhists and other religious groups (27.80 per cent) have higher percentage of matriculates. Among caste groups, the ratios are generally higher of matriculates and other higher stages among the higher castes and lower among the Schedule Castes and Schedule Tribes. This is particularly so at higher level.

Causes of Drop-out

People who left school or education were asked about the causes of drop-out at various stages of education. Table 3.11 shows that the dominant cause 75.42 per cent is poverty or search of job. Drop-out on account of migration is 7.36 per cent. Lack of permanent settlement and language problem biding to migration are the additional reasons for discontinuing education.

TABLE 3.11 : DISTRIBUTION OF POPULATION BY REASON OF DROP-OUT

Causes	*Population*	*%*	*M*	*F*	*% M*	*% F*
Search of job, poverty	1066	75.08	804	262	75.42	24.58
Marriage	79	5.50	13	66	16.45	83.55
Migration	106	7.36	51	55	48.11	51.99
Lack of parental interest	64	4.44	26	38	40.62	59.38
Death of parents/brother or ill-health of father	56	3.89	32	24	57.14	42.86
Other causes	68	4.72	49	19	67.64	32.36
Total	1439	100.00	975	465		

Note: M = male; F = female.

Marriage was the cause for 5.50 per cent of the drop-outs. Nearly 84 per cent of girls left education due to their marriage. Lower female age at marriage is responsible for their dropping out of schools. About 4.44 per cent people left education due to lack of parents' interest and 4.72 per cent left for other causes. Other causes include long distance of school, lack of facilities in school, failure and other.

This shows that although poverty is an important cause for drop-outs, some causes are male-specific and some female-specific. Male-specific causes are poverty, search of job (75.42 per cent), death of parents, brother or ill-health of father (57.14 per cent) and others (67.64 per cent). Female-specific causes are marriage (83.55 per cent) and lack of parents' interest (59.38 per cent).

Summing up

The squatter population is mainly Hindus followed by Muslims. The share of other religious groups is around one per cent only. The imbalance in terms of caste category is, however, quite evident. More than half of the squatter population compares Scheduled Castes, followed by Other Backward Classes (OBC) and higher castes. The sex ratio is generally lower than the national average. It is particularly low among the Other Backward Classes and Schedule Tribes. The age structure also revealed significant imbalances. More than 40 per cent of the people are below 15 years and 3.60 per cent more than 60 years. This age composition drops drastically in favour of the young age group. Thus the dependency on young people is very high. The sex ratio as well as the age structure seems to be greatly influenced by migration. While for the males migration is induced for relatively young persons by employment female migration is both due to marriage and employment.

Marital status is also influenced by sex migration. Unmarried persons outnumber the married. More males among the married are literate but the literacy rate is lower among the Muslims. It is also low among the Scheduled Castes and Other Backward Classes as compared to higher castes.

Educationally, the major concentration is primary and middle level. A very small number reach higher level, particularly among the Scheduled Castes and Scheduled Tribes. The search for job and poverty are the dominant reasons for drop-out at various stages. Marriage and migration are other reasons for dropping out. Poverty, search of job, death of parents or ill-health of father are male-specific causes; while marriage and lack of parents' interest are female-specific causes.

CHAPTER 4

Squatter Migration

Out of the total 1449 squatter households, 1407 heads of households have migrated to Delhi, and the remaining 42 were born here. Hence, the analysis about migrational characteristics pertains to 1407 households. The information about the migrants is fairly comprehensive and covers aspects like place of origin, causes of migration, year of leaving home and arrival in Delhi, age at the time of migration, step-migration, contact in migration and occupational mobility in migration.

Place of Origin

The migrants have come from different states of India as well as from neighbouring countries. (Table 4.1). Most of the households are from Uttar Pradesh (41.86 per cent) followed by Bangladesh (22.38 per cent), Bihar (12.43 per cent) and West Bengal (12.15 per cent). These four source regions contributed more than 85 per cent of the migrants. The rest of the migrants are from Madhya Pradesh (3.77 per cent), Haryana (2.06 per cent), Rajasthan (2.84 per cent), Punjab (0.42 per cent), Orissa (0.36 per cent), Himachal Pradesh (0.21 per cent), Pakistan (0.35 per cent), Tamil Nadu (0.14 per cent) and elsewhere (0.99 per cent).

More than one-fourth of the migrants are from Bangladesh and Pakistan. The division of the Indian subcontinent has brought large-scale migration amongst the countries of the region. The Bangladesh war, riots and communal tensions resulted in large scale migration to India.

Of the total 1260 Hindu migrants, about 37.00 per cent are from Uttar Pradesh, 24.76 per cent from Bangladesh, 12.93

TABLE 4.1 : PERCENTAGE DISTRIBUTION OF MIGRANTS BY PLACE OF ORIGIN

Native place	*No. of migrant households*	*Percentage*
Bihar	175	12.43
Haryana	29	2.06
Himachal Pradesh	3	0.21
Madhya Pradesh	53	3.77
Orissa	5	0.36
Punjab	6	0.42
Rajasthan	40	2.84
Tamil Nadu	2	0.14
Uttar Pradesh	589	41.86
West Bengal	171	12.15
Bangladesh	315	22.38
Pakistan	5	0.35
Other places	14	0.99
Total	1407	100

per cent from Bihar and 13.09 per cent from West Bengal (Table 4.2) . Thus these four regions account for about 82.16 per cent of the total Hindu migrants. Muslim migrants are mainly from Uttar Pradesh (83.72 per cent), Bihar (8.53 per cent), Rajasthan (3.10 per cent) and West Bengal (3.88 per cent). Christian migrants are from Uttar Pradesh (40.0 per cent) and 20 per cent each from Madhya Pradesh, West Bengal and Bangladesh. Sikh migrants are from Uttar Pradesh (87.5 per cent) and Haryana (12.5 per cent). Buddhists and other minor religious groups come mostly from Bangladesh (about 40 per cent) and Uttar Pradesh (about 20 per cent).

Among the Scheduled Caste migrants, 31.88 per cent are from Uttar Pradesh, 31.18 per cent from Bangladesh, 15.52 per cent from West Bengal and 9.72 per cent from Bihar (Table 4.3). Among the Scheduled Tribe migrants, 26.66 per cent each are from Uttar Pradesh and Rajasthan, 13.33 per cent each from West Bengal and Bihar and 6.66 per cent each from Madhya Pradesh, Bangladesh and Haryana. Among the migrants of higher castes, 36.42 per cent are from Uttar Pradesh, 22.0 per cent are from Bangladesh and 21.07 per cent from Bihar. The majority of the migrants of other backward classes belong to Uttar Pradesh, followed by Bihar and Bangladesh.

TABLE 4.2 : RELIGION-BASED DISTRIBUTION OF HOUSEHOLDS BY PLACE OF ORIGIN (PERCENTAGE)

State / country	*Hindu*	*Muslin*	*Christian*	*Sikh*	*Buddhist*	*Total*
Bihar	93.14	6.28	—	—	0.57	175
	(12.93)	(8.53)			(20.00)	
Uttar Pradesh	80.00	18.33	0.34	1.18	0.17	589
	(37.38)	(83.72)	(40.00)	(87.5)	(20.00)	
Madhya Pradesh	98.11	—	1.88	—	—	53
	(4.12)		(20.0)			
Rajasthan	90.00	10.00	—	—	—	40
	(2.85)	(3.10)				
Tamil Nadu	100.00	—	—	—	—	2
	(0.15)					
Punjab	100.00	—	—	—	—	6
	(0.47)					
West Bengal	96.5	2.92	0.58	—	—	171
	(13.09)	(3.88)	(20.00)			
Bangladesh	99.04	—	0.33	—	0.63	315
	(24.76)		(20.00)		(40.00)	
Haryana	96.55	—	—	3.44	—	29
	(2.22)			(12.5)		
Orissa	100.00	—	—	—	—	5
	(0.40)					
Himachal Pradesh	100.00	—	—	—	—	3
	(0.23)					
Pakistan	100.0	—	—	—	—	5
	(0.40)					
Other places	85.71	7.14	—	—	7.14	14
	(0.95)	(0.77)			(20.00)	
Total	1260	129	5	8	5	1407

Note: Figures in the first column indicate percentage share of each religion to total migrant from the individual state, while the second column the percentages share of state in total migrants from religion.

Causes of Migration

Information regarding causes of migration has been grouped under seven heads, viz. education, employment, marriage, family moved, partition, war or communal violence, came with husband, flood and other causes. The category "others" includes

TABLE 4.3 : CASTE-WISE DISTRIBUTION OF MIGRANTS BY PLACE OF ORIGIN

Place of origin	*SC*	*%*	*ST*	*%*	*Higher caste*	*%*	*OBC*	*%*	*Total*
Bihar	70	9.79	2	13.33	59	21.07	32	12.8	163
Uttar Pradesh	228	31.88	4	26.66	102	36.42	137	54.8	471
Madhya Pradesh	29	4.05	1	6.66	7	2.5	15	6.0	52
Rajasthan	21	2.93	4	26.66	3	1.07	8	3.2	36
Tamil Nadu	0	0	0	0	1	0.35	1	0.4	2
Punjab	4	0.55	0	0	2	0.71	0	0	6
West Bengat	111	15.52	2	13.33	32	11.42	20	8.0	165
Bangtadesh	223	31.18	1	6.66	63	22.5	25	10.0	312
Haryana	18	2.51	1	6.66	3	1.07	6	2.4	28
Orissa	4	0.55	0	0	1	0.35	0	0	5
Himachal Pradesh	2	0.27	0	0	1	0.35	0	0	3
Pakistan	1	0.14	0	0	2	0.71	2	0.8	5
Other places	4	0.55	0	0	4	1.42	4	1.6	12
Total	715	100	15	100	280	100	250	100	1260

Note: SC = Scheduled Castes; ST = Scheduled Tribes; OBC = Other Backward Classes.

minor causes like social disturbances, fight with family, accompanying brother, etc. (see Table 4.4).

Employment was the cause of migration for more than three-fourths of the respondents. Partition, war, riot or communal violence caused the migration of 12.36 per cent of respondents.

TABLE 4.4 : PERCENTAGE DISTRIBUTION OF MIGRANTS BY CAUSES OF MIGRATION

Cause of migration	*Households*	*% of total households*
Education	2	0.14
Employment	1077	76.54
Marriage	16	1.13
Family moved	116	8.24
Partition, war, riots	174	12.36
Came with husbands	1	0.07
Flood	10	0.71
Other causes	11	0.78
Total	1407	100

Among the rest, 8.24 per cent migrated due to family movement to Delhi, 1.13 per cent due to marriage and 0.71 per cent due to flood. A very small proportion (0.14 per cent) migrated for educational purposes.

To know whether there exists any association between causes of migration and place of origin, the migrant have been cross-classified by state of origin (Table 4.5). It shows that migration due to partition, war and communal violence is region-specific. Of the total 174 households, 97.12 per cent came from Bangladesh, others are from Uttar Pradesh, Pakistan and from "other places". Migration due to displacement caused by flood also shows that migrants came from Bihar (20 per cent), West Bengal (30 per cent), Uttar Pradesh (20 per cent), Bangladesh (10 per cent) and Madhya Pradesh (10 per cent). In these states floods create massive destruction of settlements and property and this ultimately leads to outmigration.

Most of those who migrated on account of marriage are from Uttar Pradesh (68.25 per cent) and the rest from West Bengal, Bangladesh and Madhya Pradesh. With the exception of Bangladesh, employment-induced migration was the main reason. Employment in fact was the sole cause of migration from Orissa, Tamil Nadu and Himachal Pradesh. From Bangladesh, the majority of the migration has taken place due to riot and partition, and the share of employment-induced migration is thus low.

Period of Migration

The year of migration is an important aspect of the study of migration. For this purpose, the year of leaving home was classified into four periods, i.e. before 1970, during 1970–80, 1980–90 and after 1991. Of the total 1407 heads of the household, one-fourth migrated before 1970 (Table 4.6). The majority (56.07 per cent) migrated during the period 1970–80. The proportion of migrants during the decade 1980–90 was comparatively small (18.62 per cent). The proportion of migrants during 1990–92 was obviously small, as this survey was itself conducted in 1992. In sum, the majority of migrants had arrived before 1980 and have been staying for a long period ranging from ten to twenty years.

TABLE 4.5 : CROSS CLASSIFICATION OF THE CAUSES OF MIGRATION WITH PLACE OF ORIGIN

State/ country	*Causes of Migration (in percentages)*							
	Edu-cation	*Employ-ment*	*Marriage*	*Family moved*	*Partition/ War/Riots*	*Flood*	*Others*	*Total*
Bihar		94.28 (15.22)		3.42 (5.17)	0.57 (0.57)	1.71 (30.00)		175 (12.43)
Haryana		86.20 (2.32)		10.34 (2.58)			3.44 (9.09)	29 (2.06)
HP	100 (0.27)							3 (0.21)
MP	1.88 (50.00)	84.90 (4.17)	1.88 (6.25)	9.43 (4.31)		1.88 (0.00)		53 (3.77)
Orissa		100 (0.46)						5 (0.36)
Punjab		83.33 (0.46)		16.66 (0.86)				6 (0.42)
Rajasthan		87.50 (3.24)		12.5 (4.31)				40 (2.94)
Tamil Nadu		100.0 (0.18)						2 (0.14)
UP		88.96 (48.65)	1.86 (68.25)	7.47 (37.93)	0.16 (0.57)	0.33 (20.0)	1.01 (54.54)	589 (41.86)

State/ country	*Causes of Migration (in percentages)* *Edu- cation*	*Employ- ment*	*Marriage*	*Family moved*	*Partition/ War/Riots*	*Flood*	*Others*	*Total*
West Bengal	0.58	85.96	1.16	8.77		1.75	1.75	171
	(50.0)	(13.64)	(12.5)	(12.93)		(30.0)	(27.27)	(12.15)
Bangladesh		33.33	0.63	11.74	53.69	0.31	0.31	315
		(9.74)	(12.5)	(31.89)	(97.12)	(10.0)	(9.09)	(22.38)
Pakistan		60.0			40.0			5
		(0.27)			(1.14)			(0.35)
Other places		92.85			7.14			14
		(1.20)			(0.57)			(0.99)
Total	3	1077	16	116	174	10	11	1407

Note: Figures in the first column indicate percentage on the horizontal total and those in second column within the bracket indicate percentage on vertical total.

Table 4.6 also shows the year of arrival in Delhi. While about 25.09 per cent of the migrants left their home, only 13.66 per cent of them arrived in Delhi. During 1970–80 while 56.07 per cent people left home, about 61.00 per cent people arrived in Delhi. It means more people arrived in Delhi than those who departed from their home. Yearly information on arrival and departure of the households shows that during 1980–87 more people arrived in Delhi than departed. This indicates a process of step-migration.

TABLE 4.6 : DISTRIBUTION OF MIGRANTS BY YEAR OF LEAVING HOME AND ARRIVAL IN DELHI (YEAR OF SURVEY 1992)

	Year of leaving and arrival in Delhi	*House-holds left Home*	*%*	*Households arrived in Delhi*	*%*
1.	Before 1970	353	25.09	188	13.36
2.	1970-1980	789	56.07	865	61.48
3 (i)	1981	99	7.03	134	9.52
(ii)	1982	31	2.20	43	3.05
(iii)	1983	29	2.06	43	3.05
(iv)	1984	33	2.34	42	3.00
(v)	1985	24	1.70	28	2.00
(vi)	1986	21	1.50	26	1.84
(vii)	1987	13	0.92	16	1.13
(viii)	1988	6	0.42	6	0.42
(ix)	1989	4	0.28	11	0.78
(x)	1990	2	0.14	2	0.14
4.	1981-1990	262	18.62	351	24.94
5.	After 1991	3	0.21	3	0.21
	Total	1407	100	1407	100

To find whether there exists any association between the place of origin and period of leaving home, the information is cross-classified in Table 4.7. The table shows that the majority of the migrants from Bangladesh and all migrants from Pakistan migrated before 1970. In this period, no migration took place from Orissa and Punjab. During period 1970–80, when migration into Delhi was the highest, the highest ingress was from Haryana (75.86 per cent), followed by West Bengal (63.15 per cent), Uttar Pradesh (60.78 per cent) and Bihar (61.14 per cent). In this period, migration from Orissa was 40.0 per

TABLE 4.7 : PERCENTAGE DISTRIBUTION OF MIGRANTS BY PLACE OF ORIGIN AND YEAR OF MIGRATION

Place of origin	*Before 1970*	*1970–80*	*1980–90*	*After 1990*
Bihar	10.85 (5.38)	61.14 (13.56)	27.42 (18.32)	0.57 (33.33)
Haryana	6.89 (0.56)	75.86 (2.78)	17.24 (1.90)	—
Himachal Pradesh		66.66 (0.25)	33.33 (0.38)	—
Madhya Pradesh	15.09 (2.26)	56.60 (3.80)	26.41 (5.34)	1.88 (33.33)
Orissa	—	40.0 (0.25)	60.0 (1.14)	—
Punjab	—	33.33 (0.25)	66.66 (1.52)	—
Rajasthan	27.5 (3.11)	55.0 (2.78)	17.5 (2.67)	—
Tamil Nadu	50.0 (0.28)	—	50.0 (0.38)	—
Uttar Pradesh	19.86 (33.14)	60.78 (45.37)	19.18 (43.12)	0.17 (33.33)
West Bengal	7.60 (3.68)	63.15 (13.68)	29.23 (19.08)	—
Bangladesh	54.60 (48.72)	40.63 (16.22)	4.76 (5.72)	—
Pakistan	100.0 (1.41)	—	—	—
Other places	35.71 (1.41)	57.14 (1.01)	7.14 (0.38)	—
Total	353	789	262	—

Note: Figures in the first column indicate percentage of the migrant in each period to total migrant from the state, while those in bracket show the percentage share of each state in total, for each period.

cent, 33.33 per cent from Punjab and 40.0 per cent from Bangladesh. During 1980–90, the trend of migration declined except from Orissa and Punjab, these two states accounting for the highest ingress during this period. During 1990–92, only three households migrated, one each from Uttar Pradesh, Madhya Pradesh and Bihar.

Possible association between the cause of migration and period of leaving home is cross-classified in Table 4.8. The table shows a strong association between these two aspects. Employment being the main cause of migration, most of the migration has taken place during 1970–80. In the years before 1970, only 16 per cent, and between 1980–90, only 22.09 per cent migrants left home. Migration due to marriage shows that 43.75 per cent of the migration has taken place before 1970, 50.0 per cent in 1970–80 and about 6.25 per cent during 1980–90. In the case of family movement, 41.73 per cent migrated before 1970, 46.08 per cent in 1970–80 and only 12.17 per cent in 1980–90.

TABLE 4.8 : PERCENTAGE DISTRIBUTION OF MIGRANTS BY CAUSES OF MIGRATION AND YEAR OF LEAVING HOME

Cause of migration	*Before 1970*	*1970–80*	*1980–90*	*After 1990*	*Total*
Education	—	50.0	50.0	—	2
		(0.12)	(0.38)		(0.14)
Employment	16.80	60.81	22.09	0.27	1077
	(51.27)	(83.01)	(90.83)	(100.0)	(76.54)
Marriage	43.75	50.0	6.25	—	16
	(1.98)	(1.01)	(0.38)		(1.13)
Family moved	41.73	46.08	12.17	—	115
	(13.59)	(6.71)	(5.34)		(8.24)
Partition, war, riot	62.64	35.05	2.29	—	174
	(30.87)	(7.73)	(1.52)		(12.36)
Came with	100	—	—		1
husband	(10.28)				(0.07)
Flood	27.27	54.54	18.18		11
	(0.84)	(0.76)	(0.76)		(0.71)
Other causes	36.36	45.45	18.18		11
	(1.13)	(0.63)	(0.76)		(0.71)
Total	353	789	262	3	1407

Note: Figures in the first column show the horizontal percentage and figures in the brackets show the vertical percentage.

Migration due to riot, partition and war shows a strong association with the period of migration. 62.64 per cent of the migrants left home before 1970, 35.05 per cent during 1970–80 and only 2.29 per cent during 1980–90. Flood also caused migration to the extent of 27.27 per cent before 1970. Flood-related migration increased during 1970–80 as about 54.75 per cent migration has taken place during the period. The trend slowed down in 1980–90, in which only 18.18 per cent migration has taken place.

The discussion indicates that there is a strong association between the period of migration and causes of migration. While most migrants left home during 1970–80 for employment, due to flood, family movement and marriage, before 1970, partition, war, riot and family movement caused most of the migration.

Age at Time of Migration

Table 4.9 gives information regarding the age of the head of the household at the time of migration. The table shows that of the 1407 migrants, more than 65 per cent migrated before 24 years of age. Detailed analysis of age-wise data further reveals that 21.32 per cent of the migrants migrated before the age of 15 years, 45.20 per cent migrated between the age of 15 and 24 years and 20.18 per cent between 25 and 34 years of age. This shows that one-fourth of the migrants were child labourers or minors at the time of migration. Only 7.82 per cent of the people migrated between 35 and 44 years of age. We thus observe that as the age increases, the proportion of migrants decrease. In the age group of 45–59 years, only 5.12 per cent of the total migrants migrated; and in the age group of 60 years and above only 0.35 per cent people migrated.

TABLE 4.9 : AGE OF THE HEAD OF THE HOUSEHOLD AT THE TIME OF MIGRATION

Age group	*No. of migrants*	*Percentage*
< 15 years	300	21.32
15-24 years	636	45.20
25-34 years	284	20.18
35-44 years	110	7.82
45-59 years	72	5.12
60 and above	5	0.35
Total	1407	100.00

To find out whether there exists any association between the age of migrants and the causes of their migration, these two variables are cross-classified in the Table 4.10. The table shows that people's migration for education is mainly determined by the age factor. In the case of employment, as the age of the migrants increased, their number decreased. The job market looks for young people, so employment-related migration decreased along with increase in age. Information on marriage migration shows that, of the 16 migrants, about 19 per cent migrated below 15 years of age and 56.25 per cent between the age of 15 and 24 years. While 6.24 per cent migrated between 25 and 34 years of age, no one migrated in the age of 35–44 years under this category. About 19.00 per cent of the respondents in the age group of 45–59 years migrated due to marriage. The marriage migration in the higher age group may be because of second marriage or widow remarriage.

In case of family movement, most of the migrants (70.69 per cent) migrated before the age of 15 year, the respondents being dependent children at that time. Due to partition, war, riot or communal violence, more than one-third of the migrants left home before 15 years of age and another 25.86 per cent migrated at the age of 15–24 years. After the age of 25, migration decreased. It is found that people affected by partition, war or riot left home at an early age but came to Delhi at a later age because their employment needs were satisfied in Dandkaranaya and in other places where they were first resettled by the Indian government.

For flood-induced migration, there is no consistent pattern on the age of the migration. Of the 10 such migrants, 2 migrated before 15 years of age, 4 between 15–25 years of age, 1 in 25–34 years of age, 2 in 35–44 years of age and another 1 in the age of 45–59 years. As flood causes havoc and destroys settlements and cultivable lands, people of any age group choose to migrate.

Direct/step-wise Migration

Migration has taken place both directly and step-wise; the mode being determined by circumstances, information and distance between place of departure and destination. Information

TABLE 4.10 : PERCENTAGE DISTRIBUTION OF MIGRANTS OF DIFFERENT AGE GROUPS ACCORDING TO THE CAUSES OF MIGRATION

Age group	*Education*	*Employment*	*Marriage*	*Family moved*	*Partition / War / Riots*	*Came with husband*	*Flood*	*Other causes*	*Total*
< 15 years	0.33 (50.0)	49.33 (13.74)	1.00 (18.75)	27.33 (70.69)	20.33 (35.06)		0.66 (20.0)	1.00 (27.27)	300
15-24 years	0.16 (50.0)	86.63 (51.16)	1.41 (56.25)	3.30 (18.1)	7.07 (25.86)	0.16 (100.0)	0.63 (40.0)	0.63 (36.36)	636
25-34 years		82.40 (21.73)	0.35 (6.25)	2.81 (6.9)	13.02 (21.26)		0.35 (10.0)	1.05 (27.27)	284
35-44 years		87.54 (8.63)		0.90 (0.86)	11.81 (7.47)		1.81 (20.0)	0.90 (9.09)	110
45-59 years		69.44 (4.64)	4.17 (18.75)	5.55 (3.44)	19.44 (8.04)		1.39 (10.0)		72
60 and above		20.0 (0.09)			80.0 (2.30)				5
Total	2	1077	16	116	174	1	10	11	1407

Note: Figures in the first column show the horizontal percentage and those in the bracket shows the vertical percentage.

regarding direct or step-wise migration was collected by ascertaining information about the number of places the respondent had stayed before moving to Delhi (see Table 4.11).

Of the total 1407 migrants, three-fourths came directly to Delhi, 19.97 per cent stayed at one place before coming to Delhi, 3.55 per cent stayed at two different places, 0.92 per cent stayed at three places and 0.63 per cent stayed at more than three places.

TABLE 4.11 : DISTRIBUTION OF MIGRANTS BY STEP-WISE MIGRATION

Step-wise migration		*Number of respondents*	*Percentage*
Came directly		1054	74.92
Stayed at:	one place	281	19.97
	two places	50	3.55
	three places	13	0.92
	more than three places	9	0.63
Total		1407	100

To find whether there exists any association between the place of origin and step-migration, information on these two aspects has been cross-tabulated in Table 4.12. It is seen from the table that the proportion of direct migration decreased as the distance from Delhi increased a phenomenon which Ravenstein calls "distance decay".[1] Although the actual distance of the places is not known, the location of the state indicates the distance decay proposition. Migration was direct for migrants from Haryana, Punjab, Himachal Pradesh (all neighbouring states of Delhi) and Tamil Nadu. The incidence of direct migration was 90–100 per cent for migrants from Uttar Pradesh, Madhya Pradesh and Rajasthan and 80–90 per cent for Bihar, West Bengal and Orissa. As against this, 60 per cent migrants from Pakistan and 26.60 per cent from Bangladesh came directly to Delhi.

Thus about 55 per cent migrants from Bangladesh, 40 per cent from Pakistan, 20 per cent from Orissa, 16 per cent from West Bengal, 8 per cent from Uttar Pradesh and 2.5 per cent from Rajasthan stayed at one place before coming to Delhi. Migrants from Bihar and Uttar Pradesh stayed at three places.

TABLE 4.12 : PERCENTAGE DISTRIBUTION OF MIGRANTS BY STEP-WISE MIGRATION AND PLACE OF ORIGIN

State / country	*Came directly*	*One place*	*Two places*	*Three places*	*More than three places*	*Total*
Bihar	85.71	10.28	2.85	1.14	0	175
Uttar Pradesh	90.15	8.65	1.01	0.16	0	589
Madhya Pradesh	96.22	3.77	0	0	0	53
Rajasthan	97.50	2.50	0	0	0	40
Tamil Nadu	100.00	0.00	0	0	0	2
Punjab	100.00	0.00	0	0	0	6
West Bengal	83.04	16.95	0	0	0	171
Bangladesh	26.66	54.92	12.38	3.17	2.85	315
Haryana	100.00	0.00	0	0	0	29
Orissa	80.00	20.00	0	0	0	5
Himachal Pradesh	100.00	0.00	0	0	0	3
Pakistan	60.00	40.0	0	0	0	5
Other places	71.42	28.57	0	0	0	14
Total	75.0	19.97	3.55	0.92	0.64	1407

Migrants from Bangladesh stayed at more than three places before reaching Delhi, from their places of settlement in Bihar, West Bengal and Dandakaranya region by the Government.

Contact in Migration

The process of migration is always controlled by circumstances, and information about the opportunities available. Although not always, people in migration came through some contact. It is observed that "arrival of the rural migrants in the city is not due to random search for employment but largely depends on the presence of friends, castemen, relations, fellow villagers or those from neighbouring areas".[2] Information regarding contact in migration is given in Table 4.13. It is seen from the table that 55.16 per cent of the migrants came through contacts. Nearly half of them came through family contacts, and about one-fourth each through relatives and other connections. It may also be noted that nearly 45 per cent of the migrants came through without any contact.

To find out as to whether any association exists between the

TABLE 4.13 : CONTACT IN MIGRATION

Types of contact	*Number of migrants*	*Percentage*
No contact	631	44.84
Contact exists	775	55.16
Family	199	14.14
Relative	371	26.43
Others	205	14.57
Total	1406	100.00

causes of migration and contact in migration, the two variables are cross-classified in Table 4.14. Not surprisingly, the table shows that in the case of forced migration, like flood, partition, riot or communal violence, the percentage of migrants without any contact is more. It is 68.40 per cent in case of partition and riot, and 60 per cent in case of flood. But those who came through contact, about half had relatives in Delhi and, about a quarter came through other family connections. In the case of induced migration, however around 60 per cent came through contacts. Of these, who came for employment, 48 per cent came through relatives, 24 per cent through family and 27 per cent came through other than family and relatives. Majumdar observes that "in urban areas, recruitment into occupations takes place in an informal manner. Vacancies are advertised by word of mouth and therefore territorial, kin and caste affinities play a predominant role in the recruitment of workers".[3] Thus though the migrants may move to the city individually, they are not among strangers but are supported by a network of social relations built on ties of kin, caste, regional affinities and friendship.

Summing Up

People from various states and neighbouring countries (Bangladesh and Pakistan) migrated to the squatter colonies at different points of time. A big share of migrants is from Uttar Pradesh, followed by Bangladesh, Bihar and West Bengal. These four states have contributed 86 per cent of the migrant

TABLE 4.14 : TYPES OF CONTACT OF MIGRANTS BY CAUSES OF MIGRATION

Type of Contact	*Edu-cation*	*Employ-ment*	*Marriage*	*Family moved*	*Partition / War / Riots*	*Came with husband*	*Flood*	*Other causes*	*Total*
No contact	N	437 (40.58)	4 (25.0)	61 (52.58)	119 (68.40)	N	6 (60.0)	4 (36.36)	631 (44.8%)
Family	N	157 (24)	4 (14.58)	23 (25.0)	12 (23%) (19.82)	N	N	3 (6.90)	199 (14.1%)
Relative	1 (50.0)	310 (48)	5 (28.78)	26 (31.25)	24 (48%) (22.41)	1 (13.8)	2 (100.0)	3 (20.0)	372 (26.45)
Other than family/ retative	1 (27)	173 (50.0)	3 (16.06)	6 (18.75)	19 (5.17)	N (10.9)	2 (20.0)	1 (9.10)	205 (14.6%)
Total	2	1077	16	116	174	1	10	11	14.0

Note: N for Nil.

households, with Uttar Pradesh accounting for as much as 41 per cent of the total migrants. The other migrant households are from Madhya Pradesh, Haryana, Rajasthan, Punjab, Orissa, Himachal Pradesh, Tamil Nadu and other states. Of the total households, 21 per cent have migrated from Bangladesh and Pakistan. The division of the Indian subcontinent followed by war and riots are the main causes of migrations from these two countries.

Employment accounts for more than three-fourths of the migration. Partition, war and riot were the second most important cause. Other causes are family movement, marriage, flood and education.

The majority of the migration (56.7 per cent) took place during 1970–80, followed by 1980–90 and the period before 1970. After 1981, the tempo of migration has decreased. Migration before the 1970s is mostly from Bangladesh and Pakistan, and during 1970–80 is from Uttar Pradesh, West Bengal, Bihar and Haryana. Between 1980–90 the migration was mostly from Orissa and Punjab. It is noticed that there is a time dimension to migration. Migration for employment has mostly taken place during 1970–80. In case of riot, partition etc., most of it has occurred before 1970.

The migrants' age profile indicates that most of them migrated before 25 years of age (66.34 per cent), of which 21.32 per cent migrated before 15 years of age and the remaining 45.2 per cent between 15 and 24 years of age. Beyond the age of 35, the number of migrants decreased as the age increased. The causes of migration are closely interlinked with the age of the migrants. The proportion of migrants in search of employment, education, or marriage generally decreased as the age increased. In case of migration due to flood, partition, war, riot, etc., the migration obviously takes place irrespective of the age factor.

Three-fourths of the migrants came directly to Delhi. The rest coming in step-wise migration. Distance seems to play an important role in step-wise migration. The migrants from nearby states like Haryana, Rajasthan and Punjab, Himachal Pradesh migrated directly, the only exception being households from a far-off state like Tamil Nadu, who also migrated directly to Delhi. Step-wise migration was prominent in case of migration from Bangladesh.

More than half of the respondents migrate through contacts. The connection through relative and family has played a major role in developing contact. This is particularly so in migration for employment.

NOTES

1. M. Hussain, 1994. *Human Geography*, Rawat Publication, Jaipur, pp. 18–150.
2. Tapas K. Majumdar, 1978. The Urban Poor and Social change—A study to Squatter Settlements in Delhi, De Souza, A. (ed.), *The Indian City Poverty, Ecology and Urban Development*, Manohar Publishers, New Delhi, pp. 40–1.
3. T.K. Majumdar, op. cit.

CHAPTER 5

Economic Condition

People of squatter settlements are a conglomeration of different castes and religions, coming from different regions. In their current habitat they live in a diversified and complex economic set-up. The economic characteristics of squatters have been a major concern of study. For the present study information was collected from the heads of the households and their occupational and employment status was analysed for status as workers and non-workers, main and marginal workers, work participation rate, household income, per capita income, level of poverty and distance of workplace.

Work Participation Rate

The census of India (1981) defined work as participation, physical or mental, in any economically productive activity. Work involves, besides actual work, effective supervision of work. By taking the census definition of work, people are classified in to workers and non-workers. People doing household duties, students, dependants, retired persons or rentiers, beggars, inmates of institutions are included in the category of non-workers.

Table 5.1 lists information about work participation rate (WPR) by gender, religion and caste groups. WPR of the total population is 31.52 per cent, 45.47 per cent for males and only 15.42 per cent for females.

There is some difference in WPR across the religious groups. WPR is higher than average of for the Christians and lowest among the Muslims. WPR for caste groups does not differ significantly from the average. Regarding female WPR, it is

TABLE 5.1 : WORK PARTICIPATION RATES OF PERSONS, MALES AND FEMALES AND MALE-FEMALE DISPARITY IN WORK PARTICIPATION RATE BY RELIGION AND CASTE-WISE

Religion / caste	*Total workers*	*Total*	*Male*	*Female*
All	2071	31.52	45.47	15.42
Hindu	1871	31.92	45.14	16.47
Muslim	174	28.01	48.89	6.25
Christian	8	36.36	65.54	18.18
Sikh	10	23.0	37.50	5.55
Buddhist and others	8	33.33	45.46	36.07
Scheduled Castes	1093	32.30	44.76	18.21
Scheduled Tribes	23	31.50	40.47	19.35
Higher Castes	405	31.41	45.74	14.76
OBCs	350	31.39	45.85	12.73
All	1871			

Note: * Male–female disparity has been calculated on the basis of Sopher's Index of Gender disparity.

argued that "women's participation in economic activity is determined among other things, by factors like marital status, number of children they have to take care of, the additional income they can earn and, above all, the social outlook about female employment."[3] Overall male-female WPR disparity is 0.66. Disparity was high among Muslims (the highest), Sikhs and Christians and low among Hindus and Buddhists. Among the caste groups, male-female disparity in WPR was the highest among the other backward classes, followed by higher castes. It was low among the Scheduled tribes followed by Scheduled castes (see Table 5.2). It is seen from Table 5.2 the WPR for both males and females and total increase with increase in per capita income, indicating a direct relationship between the two.

Occupational Pattern

Given their low educational level and skill workers from the squatter settlements tend to be engaged in low-paid unskilled work like porters, loaders, rickshaw-pullers, cooks, construction workers, low-grade employees in public undertakings, government and semi-government agencies and private offices

TABLE 5.2 : WORK PARTICIPATION RATES OF TOTAL PERSONS, MALES AND FEMALES AND MALE-FEMALE DISPARITY BY PER CAPITA INCOME

Per capita income	*Work Participation Rate*			
	Persons	*Males*	*Females*	*Male-Female disparity*
1-65	19.35	28.39	9.46	0.580
65-125	19.96	31.54	9.50	0.642
125-180	31.98	35.63	11.80	0.616
180-280	30.17	43.52	16.85	0.580
280-370	38.38	52.78	20.74	0.630
370-500	42.80	61.54	22.28	0.74
500-1500	61.01	78.76	31.17	0.91
> 1500	50.0	77.78	0.0	
All income groups	31.52	45.46	15.42	

as peons and watchmen: Among the other occupations are: petty traders and vendors; carpenters, blacksmiths, leather workers; and semi-professional jobs like compounders, school teachers, clerks and accountants, etc. The range of occupations is more than 120. For analytical convenience these are clubbed into 45 groups and further into eight broad groups.

Among the 2071 workers shown in Table 5.3 only two occupations have more than 150 persons engaged in them. These are, factory workers and casual labourers. Higher factory employment is mainly due to the locational factor of the squatter settlement, near the New Okhla Industrial Area. Factory jobs generally include rubber, leather, spare parts, electronic goods making, shows factory, etc. Unskilled and less educated persons first enter into casual labour, which is the other large category of employment, and later shift to other occupations depending on their educational qualifications, skill and choice of jobs. Three-fourths of the labourers in the two categories are illiterate, and one-fourth of them possess education up to middle class.

The next highest occupational categories, employing 100–150 workers, are petty trading shopkeeping and tailoring. These two occupations absorb nearly 255 persons. Domestic work and painting is the third largest occupational category, giving employment to 75–100 persons. These two occupations absorb 174 people. Domestic work is the speciality of females, most of

TABLE 5.3 : CLASSIFICATION OF WORKERS BY OCCUPATIONS

Occupation	*Number*
Factory worker, labourer	> 150
Shopkeeper, tailor	105–150
Maid-servant	75–100
Driver, mechanic, vendor	50–75
Carpenter, electrician, gardener, catering, hotel and restaurant, priest, security guard	25–50
Fisherman, rickshaw-puller, kabadi-wala	10–25
Blacksmith, barber, contractor, clerk, dhobi, stitching, shoe maker (cobbler), rag-picker, CPWD worker	5–10
Book-binder, carpenter, craftsman, goldsmith, doctor, music and orchestra, priest, postman, supervisor, service man	1–5

whom engage to supplement household income, in the nearby residential areas.

About 50 to 75 people in each category are engaged as drivers, merchants and vendors. These three occupations absorb about 12 per cent of the employed. Another 25 to 50 persons in each category are engaged in seven types of jobs—carpenter, guard, electrician, gardener, hotel and catering, helper and mason in construction work. About 8.00 per cent of the employed are absorbed in occupations like fisherman, junk dealer, peon, plumber, rickshaw puller, sweeper and salesman.

About 5 to 10 persons each are engaged in ten occupations which account for only 5.14 per cent of the total workers. These occupations are: blacksmith, barber, teacher, contractor, clerk, washerman, rag-picker, stitching, cobbler. Other occupations like book-binding, compounder, craftsman, doctor, goldsmith, singer, priest, postman, supervisor, and serviceman account for only 1.53 per cent of jobs.

To get a better insight into the occupational pattern the workers are classified by the national industrial classification (1970, see Table 5.4). Of the total workers about 4.64 per cent are engaged in agriculture, forestry, fishing and hunting. The main contribution in this group, comes from fishermen and gardeners. About 17.44 per cent of workers are engaged in manufacture, including repair work. Most of them are factory workers employed in nearby factories. The highest proportion

TABLE 5.4 : DISTRIBUTION OF WORKERS INTO INDUSTRIAL CLASSIFICATION (ONE DIGIT LEVEL)

Industrial classes	*Number of workers*	*Percentage*
Agriculture, forestry, fishing and hunting	67	4.64
Mining and quarrying	4	0.28
Manufacturing and repairing	252	17.44
Electricity, gas and water	41	2.84
Construction	285	19.73
Wholesale and retail trade and restaurants and hotels	265	18.35
Transport, storage and communication	178	12.32
Financing, insurance, real estate and business services	74	5.12
Community, social and personal services	278	19. 25
	1444	100

Note: The industrial classification is based on the National Industrial Classification (NIC) 1970.

of worker are engaged in construction (19.73 per cent). In metropolitan Delhi construction is an important activity both in the government and the private sector, calling for no major professional competence from the slum dwellers.

About 19.25 per cent workers are employed in community, social and personal services. Maid-servants, barbers, washermen, cobblers, etc., are the main contributors to this category. Next come those employed in the wholesale and retail trade, restaurant and hotel (18.35 per cent). Shopkeepers and vendors account for a major portion of workers in this category. About 12.32 per cent workers are engaged in transport, storage and communications. Drivers, mechanics and rickshaw-pullers are the main contributors to this category.

Going by sectoral division of occupations, the largest share (55.05 per cent) are employed in the tertiary sector, followed by the secondary sector (40.3 per cent). Only 4.91 per cent workers are engaged in the primary sector. The proportion in the primary and secondary sectors is higher among the Hindus and that in the tertiary sector higher among the Muslims. The Scheduled Castes predominate in the primary sector and the higher castes in the tertiary sector. The participation of other backward classes was lowest in the tertiary sector. In the secondary sector not much inter-caste difference in participation is observed. (Table 5.5)

TABLE 5.5 : DISTRIBUTION OF WORKERS INTO ECONOMIC SECTOR BY RELIGION AND CASTE GROUPS

	Primary		*Secondary*		*Tertiary*		*Total*
	Persons	*%*	*Persons*	*%*	*Persons*	*%*	
Total population	71	4.91	578	40.03	795	55.05	1444
Hindu	71	5.49	527	40.72	696	53.78	1294
Muslim	0		43	32.58	89	67.42	132
Christian	0		1	20.0	4	80.0	5
Sikh	0		5	62.5	3	37.5	8
Buddhist and other religions	0		2	40.0	3	60.0	5
Scheduled caste	26	3.52	307	41.65	404	54.81	737
Scheduled tribe	0		8	44.44	10	55.55	18
Higher caste	7	2.43	108	37.63	172	59.93	287
OBCs	38	15.08	104	41.27	110	43.65	252

Employment Status

The National Sample Survey Organisation (NSSO)[5] divides workers into four categories for purpose of employment status, viz., self-employed, regular salary/wage earner, causal labour and others. Self-employed worker are those who are engaged in their own farm or non-farm enterprises. *Salaried/wage employee* workers are those who work in others' farm or non-farm enterprises (both household and non-household) and get, in return, regular salary or wages (and not on the basis of daily or periodic renewal of work contract). *Casual labour* is engaged in others' farm or non-farm enterprises (both household and non-household) on return wages according to the terms of the daily or periodic work contract.

Information on the employment status of the sample workers is given in Table 5.6. Of the total 1442 sample workers, about 44.00 per cent are causal labourers, 30.85 per cent are self-

TABLE 5.6 : EMPLOYMENT STATUS

Religion/ caste	*Self-employed*	*Per-centage*	*Regular/ salaried/ wage employees*	*Per-centage*	*Causal labour*	*Per-centage*	*Others*	*Per-centage*	*Total*
Hindu	389	30.10	326	25.23	568	43.96	9	0.69	1292
Muslim	53	40.15	26	19.69	53	40.15	-	-	132
Christian	1	20.0	1	20.0	3	60.0	-	-	5
Sikh	1	12.5	-	-	7	87.5	-	-	8
Buddhist and other	1	20.0	-	-	4	80.0	-	-	5
Total	445	30.85	353	24.47	635	44.03	9	0.62	1442
SC	219	29.83	162	22.07	348	47.41	5	0.68	734
ST	6	33.33	2	11.11	10	55.55	-	-	18
Higher caste	97	33.79	76	26.48	110	38.32	4	1.40	287
OBCs	67	26.48	86	33.99	100	39.52	-	-	253
Total	389	30.10	326	25.23	568	43.96	9	0.69	1292

employed and 24.47 per cent are regular salaried/wage employees.

The percentage of self-employed is higher among Muslims (40.15 per cent), followed by Hindus (30.10 per cent). The ratio of self-employed is lower among other religions groups. The caste-wise distribution shows a relatively higher percentage self-employed for higher castes followed the Scheduled Castes. The other backward classes have the lowest percentage (26.48) of self-employed.

Hindus have the highest share of regular salaried/wage employees (25.23 per cent) while the Muslims account for 19.69 per cent of their working population. In caste terms, the highest percentage (33.99) are found among OBCs, followed by the higher castes (26.48 per cent) and least among the Scheduled Castes (22.07 per cent).

The opposite is the case for casual labour. The proportion of casual labour was highest among the Scheduled Tribes (55.55 per cent) and Scheduled Castes (47.41 per cent) followed by other backward classes (39.52 per cent). The ratio of casual labour among the higher castes was the lowest. The Scheduled Castes not only have a high incidence of casual labour but they also constitute nearly 61 per cent of the total casual labour.

In sum, nearly half the workforce in the squatter settlement are casual labour, and about one-third are engaged in petty self-employment. The proportion in regular salaried jobs is the lowest. The percentage of casual labour is higher among the Hindus followed by Muslims. Hindu casual labour accounts for more than 85 per cent of the total casual labour, but among the Hindus the incidence of casual labour is the highest among the Scheduled Castes and Scheduled Tribes, with the Scheduled Castes accounting for almost 61 per cent of the casual labour among the Hindus. The incidence of casual labour among the higher castes was the lowest. A greater proportion of Muslims tended to be in self-employment activities than Hindus although the gap is not wide. In the case of regular salaried employees the participation of Hindus was higher than of Muslims and other religious groups. Among the Hindus, however, the percentage of salaried earners is greater among the other backward classes and high caste worker and the lowest among the Scheduled Tribe and Scheduled Caste workers.

Distance of Work Place

Information on distance of work place was collected to understand the linkages between the nature of the economic activities and location of the squatter settlement. Our purpose is to verify whether the squatter settlement surveyed is clustered near the work place, since it is generally found that poor migrants squat at a place near their work place (Rao and Rao).[6] It is seen from Table 5.7, which gives information on the distance from work place, that about 14.63 per cent of the workers work at a distance within 5 kilometres. Nearly half of the workers (45.13 per cent) work at places 5 to 10 kilometres away from their residence. Thus 59.76 per cent of workers work within a distance of less than 10 kilometres. Among the rest, 10.42 per cent work within a distance of 10–15 kilometres, 21.32 per cent within 15–20 kilometres and the 8.48 per cent work at places more than 20 kilometres away.

Table 5.7 : Distance of Work Place

Distance km	*No. of respondents*	*Percentage*	*Cumulative in percentage*
0-5	212	14.63	14.63
5-10	654	45.13	59.76
10-15	151	10.42	70.18
15-20	309	21.32	91.50
> 20	123	8.48	100.00
Total	1449	100.00	

Table 5.8 also presents cross-classification of distance of workplace by employment status of the worker. It shows that within 5 kilometres, the proportion of self-employed workers is higher (29.43 per cent), followed by casual labourers (8.15 per cent) and regular salaried/wage employees (8.12 per cent). Self-employed persons like vendors, shopkeepers, rickshaw-pullers in fact account for about 62 per cent of the workers working within these distances. In the range between 5 and 10 kilometres, the proportion of regular salaried/wage employees is the highest (55.46 per cent) which is closely followed by casual labourers (46.23 per cent), self-employed (35.73 per cent) and other workers (22.22 per cent).

TABLE 5.8 : DISTANCE OF WORK PLACE BY EMPLOYMENT STATUS

Distance in kms	*Self employed*	*%*	*Regular salaried / wage employee*	*%*	*Casual labour*	*%*	*Others*	*%*
0–5	131	29.43	29	8.12	52	8.15	0	0.0
		(61.79)		(13.67)		(24.52)		
5–10	159	35.73	198	55.46	295	46.23	2	22.22
		(24.3)		(30.2)		(45.1)		(1.25)
10–15	25	5.61	54	15.12	71	11.12	1	11.11
		(16.5)		(35.7)		(47.0)		(4.0)
15–20	108	24.26	28	7.84	167	26.17	6	66.67
		(35.0)		(9.0)		(54.0)		(5.55)
>20	22	4.94	48	13.44	53	8.30	0	—
		(17.8)		(39.0)		(43.0)		
Total	445	100	357	100	638	100	9	100
		(30.7)		(24.6)		(44.0)		(0.77)

Note : Figures in bracket indicate horizontal percentage share

In the range between 10 and 15 kilometres, again the proportion of regular salaried and wage employees is more (15.12 per cent) followed by casual labourers (11.12 per cent) and other workers (11.11 per cent). The proportion of self-employed people (5.61 per cent) is the lowest in this distance range. The proportion of regular salaried/wage employees is also the highest (13.44 per cent) in the range of more than 20 kilometres. It is again followed by Casual Labourers (8.30 per cent) and self-employed (4.94 per cent). Thus a relatively higher proportion of regular salaried workers travel 5 to 20 kilometres distance followed by casual labour. But the regular salaried workers constitute little more than 30 per cent of the total workers in each distance range. In the case of casual workers however, not only a relatively higher proportion have to travel a distance between 5 and 20 km and above but they constitute about half of the total workers travelling in each range of 5 kilometres and above. Thus a significant proportion of casual labour have to travel relatively long distances to reach the place of work. In the range of 15–20 kilometres, however, the proportion of casual workers is the highest (26.17 per cent) followed by self-employed (24.26 per cent). Regular salaried/

wage employees' share is the lowest in this distance range. Although the percentage share of other workers is highest, their number is really low.

Migration and Occupational Change

After having examined the occupational pattern at this stage it would be relevant to know whether there is a change in occupation in the process of migration.

We observed that at the place of origin, about 32 per cent of the migrants were landless labourers, 24.5 per cent cultivators, 4.8 per cent tailors, 1.8 per cent shopkeepers and daily labourers, and 1.1 per cent factory workers. Among the other migrants, 6.10 per cent were students and 15.0 per cent were unemployed.

In the process of migration, most migrants have changed their occupations (Appendix I). Of the total 449 landless labourers, 59 continue work as daily labourers. The remaining changed their occupation. About 52 are working as factory workers, 39 have their own shops and an equal number are tailors, 28 work as painters and 24 are maid-servants. Among the cultivators about 40 persons are working as factory workers, 41 as labourers, 30 as shopkeepers, 24 as maid-servants and 17 as tailors. In the case of landless labourers and cultivators, we thus find that a few acquired some skills after migration to Delhi. Forty-nine tailors are working in the same occupation in the garment factories and in tailoring shops. Those who were students at the time of migration are currently engaged in more diversified jobs, like driver, electricians, gardener, shopkeeper, etc. In caste-based traditional occupations also a shift has taken place in the case of carpenters, washermen, fishermen, goldsmiths, blacksmiths and barbers. Most of the fishermen have also changed their occupation. Only one out of 16 fishermen continues in the same occupation. The rest have switched over to other jobs. The washermen also have changed their occupation. Half of the carpenters, however continue their original occupation.

Household Income and Per capita Income

The monthly households income has been calculated by aggregating the income of all household members from all the sources. The households have been classified into household monthly income and monthly per capita income groups. It is seen from Table 5.9 that about 5.40 per cent of households have monthly income less than Rs 500. Another 41.12 per cent have a monthly income in the range Rs 500–1000. The monthly income of most households is in this category. Thus the first two categories comprise about 46.52 per cent of the total households. The monthly income of 29.62 per cent of the households is in the range Rs 1000–1500, and another 13.00 per cent have income between Rs 1500 and 2000. Thus about 89.14 per cent of the households on an average earn less than Rs 2000 per month. The rest 10 per cent households' income varied between Rs 2000–4000 and above.

TABLE 5.9 : DISTRIBUTION OF HOUSEHOLDS BY MONTHLY HOUSEHOLD INCOME

Monthly household income (Rs)	*Households*	*Percentage*	*Cumulative percentage*
< 500	78	5.40	5.40
500–1000	594	41.12	46.52
1000–1500	428	29.62	76.14
1500–2000	185	13.00	89.14
2000–2500	84	6.00	95.14
2500–3000	34	2.35	97.49
3000–3500	22	1.52	99.01
3500–4000	6	0.41	99.42
> 4000	14	0.97	100.00
Total	1445	100.0	

Although monthly household income gives some idea about the economic well-being of the households an appropriate indicator of the level of living is per capita income. Table 5.10 gives per capita income at aggregate level by size class.

Of the total 1445 households, about 4.57 per cent have per capita income of less than Rs 95. Per capita income of 13.01 per cent is Rs 95–140 and another 15.70 per cent of persons have per capita income in the range Rs 140–180. These three categories account for one-third of the total sample households. The maximum proportion of households (29.95 per cent)

TABLE 5.10 : DISTRIBUTION OF HOUSEHOLDS BY PER CAPITA INCOME GROUPS

Per capita income (Rs)	*Households*	*Percentage*	*Cumulative percentage*
<95	66	4.57	4.57
95–140	188	13.01	17.58
140–180	227	15.70	33.28
180–280	427	29.55	62.83
280–370	177	12.25	75.08
370–500	206	14.25	89.33
500–1500	149	10.31	99.64
>1500	5	0.34	100
Total	1445	100	

however falls with in the range of Rs 180–280. This is followed by those whose per capita income falls in the range of Rs 280–370. The poverty line for urban Delhi has been fixed at per capita monthly expenditure of Rs 309 for the year 1993–94. Although we do not have data on per capita consumption expenditure, the income data at least provide some idea about the level of poverty. Assuming that consumption expenditure is mainly determined by income, the data indicate that about 66 per cent of the people have per capita income less than Rs 309. In other words approximately 66 per cent of persons in the study area live in poverty.

Summing Up

The discussion in this chapter brings out some significant features relating to the economic activities of the workers. At the overall level about 31.52 per cent of the persons participate in the economic activities. Work participation rate (WPR) is lower among the females. Further, WPR tends to be lower among households with low per capita consumption group, indicating a positive relationship between WPR and monthly per capita consumption.

The occupational structure is diversified and complex. There appears to be occupational segregation in specific occupations. The occupations which absorb most workers are casual labour, particularly in construction, factory workers, shopkeepers and vendors, tailors and maidservants. These occupations alone account for 60 per cent of the total workers.

As regards the distribution of workers among the industrial groups there are four industries which absorbed around 75 per cent of the workers. These are construction (19.73 per cent), community, social and personnel services (19.25 per cent), wholesale and retail trade (18.35 per cent) and manufacturing and repairing (17.44 per cent). Generally more workers are engaged in the tertiary sector. It is followed by secondary sector and a distant primary sector.

So far as the employment status is concerned about half of the workers are casual labourers, one-third are engaged in petty self-employment activities and remaining one-fifth are in regular salaried jobs. A high proportion of Hindus are casual labour followed by Muslims. Among the Hindus, however, the incidence of casual labour is higher among the Scheduled Castes/Tribes. In fact Scheduled Castes account for 61 per cent of the casual worker. The participation of Muslims is higher in self-employment activities and in regular salaried jobs the proportion of Hindus is higher. The ratio is particularly high among the other backward classes and high castes but low among the Scheduled Tribes and Scheduled Castes.

NOTES

1. Census of India, 1981. General Economic Tables. Part III-A(i), Registrar General of India, Ministry of Home Affairs, New Delhi, p. 37.
2. Mahendra K. Premi, A. Ramanamma and Usha Bambewala, (1983), *An Introduction to Social Demography*, Vikas Publishing House, New Delhi, p. 58
3. *Survekshana* vol. xii, no. 4, July–September 1969. A note on employment and unemployment situation in India. Dept. of Statistics, Ministry of Planning, pp. 2–5.
4. K.R. Rao and M.S.A. Rao, "Cities and Slums: A Study of a Squatters' Settlement in the City at Vijayawada", Concept Publishing Company, New Delhi, 1984, p. 3.

CHAPTER 6

Housing and Household Amenities

The present chapter seeks to evaluate the living environment of the squatter dwellers in terms of public facilities and amenities available to them. These include housing, tenure status of the building, water supply, toilet and bathing facilities, drainage system, electricity, health facilities, use of ration stops and schools.

Housing

For the vast majority of people, the type of house they live in is an important determinant of their well-being, so the quality of dwelling is an important indicator of the quality of life itself (Mathew).[1] For this purpose, along with other facilities information on housing has been collected for the squatter settlement.

Information on housing includes building material used for roof, wall and floor. According to the type of material used, the houses are classified into pucca, semi-pucca and kutcha, as per the criteria given by the National Building Organisation.[2] The basis of classification is as below:

Wall — pucca : burnt brick, G.I. sheets or other metal sheets, stone, cement, concrete.

kutcha : grass, leaves, reeds, bamboo, mud, unburnt bricks, wood.

Roof— pucca : tiles, slate, corrugated iron, zinc or other metal sheets, asbestos, cement sheets, bricks, lime and stone, stone and RBC/RCC, concrete.

kutcha : grass leaves, reeds, bamboo, thatch, mud, unburnt bricks, wood.

In addition to the material used for wall and roof, the floor of the jhuggies is also classified into kutcha or pucca. If the floor is made of mud, wood, bamboo, bricks, stone and lime, it is classified as kutcha and if it is made of cement, mosaic and tiles it is classified as pucca.

Houses of which all walls, roof and floor are made of pucca materials are classified as pucca and if all walls, roof and floor are made of kutcha materials they are classified as kutcha. If any two of the components is pucca, the house is classified as semi-pcca.

Information regarding the housing of squatter settlements reveals that more than half (52.6 per cent) of the jhuggies are kutcha (Table 6.1), one-fourth (25.5 per cent) are semi-pucca, and only 22 per cent are pucca.

TABLE 6.1 : NUMBER OF HOUSEHOLD AND PERCENTAGE OF HOUSEHOLDS OCCUPYING TYPES OF HOUSES

	No. of Households	*Percentage*
Kutcha	762	52.6
Pucca	317	21.9
Semi-Pucca	370	25.5
Total	1449	100

Detailed information on the wall, roof and floor by building material (Table 6.2) indicates that 42.5 per cent jhuggis are made of kutcha roof and 57 per cent are made of pucca material. Seven households (0.5 per cent) reported no roof at all. A major fire had broken out in the settlement before the survey (1992)

TABLE 6.2 : TYPES OF BUILDING MATERIAL USED FOR ROOF, WALL AND FLOOR

	Roof	*%*	*Wall*	*%*	*Floor*	*%*
Kutcha	616	42.7	801	55.3	763	52.7
Pucca	826	57.3	648	44.7	686	47.3
Total	1442*	100	1449	100	1449	100

* Seven houses reported no roof.

and seven households had not managed to build a roof for their house. Information on wall shows that more than half of the juggis (55.3 per cent) are made of kutcha material and rest (44.7 per cent have pucca floor.

About the tenure status of the juggis (Table 6.3) it is observed that about 99.4 per cent are self-owned and only 0.6 per cent houses are rented.

TABLE 6.3 : TENURE STATUS OF THE HOUSEHOLDS

Tenure Status	*Households*	*Percentage*
Owned	1441	99.4
Rented	8	0.6
Total	1449	100

Water Supply

There are two sources of water supply to the squatter settlement, namely tap water hand pump. Eighty-five per cent of the households depend on tap water and the remaining 15 per cent on hand pump (Table 6.4). The residents reported that the pressure of water supply remained low throughout the year and is extremely inadequate during the summer months. Water timings observed during the period of investigation were four hours in the morning (6–10 a.m.) and another two hours in the evening (4–6 p.m.). Taking the total population of the squatter settlement depending on tap water, it was found that one tap served 400 people. In the case of tube well, the population pressure is less. The ratio works out to 170 people per tube well. Long queues of children and women are a common sight before the taps. The queues start well before the water starts flowing. The struggle to get some water leads to heated argument and often to quarrels.

TABLE 6.4 : SOURCE OF DRINKING WATER

Source	*Households*	*%*	*Population*	*%*
Tap	1238	85.4	5590	84.58
Hand Pump	211	14.6	1019	15.42
Total	1449	100	6609	100

The water supply is partially augmented by the hand pumps in the settlement. However, these pumps also supply less water in the summer months. Further a single hand pump cannot take as many persons as the municipal water tap. Since water has to be drawn by manual operation, this necessitated frequent repairs, resulting in interruptions of water supply.

Toilet Facilities

Of the total 1449 households, only 18 (1.2 per cent) have their own toilet, the remaining 1431 households (98.8 per cent) being dependent on the toilet built by Sulabh International (Table 6.5). The Souchalaya is a two-storeyed building with 102 lavatory seats, 52 of them for males and 50 for females. The management charges a nominal rate of 0.25 paise per person for one use. The toilets have running water facility.

TABLE 6.5 : PLACE FOR TOILET

Place for toilet	*Households*	*Percentage*
Sulabh Sauchalay	1431	98.8
Own toilet	18	1.2
Total	1449	100

Although the toilet has 102 lavatory seats, the user-lavatory ratio is not quite favourable, with an average 130 people depending on one lavatory seat. This indicates a very high pressure of population on sanitation. This situation becomes worse in the monsoon months when the ground floor of the souchalayas is choked.

Bathing Facility

Unlike the toilets, few people use bathrooms made by Sulabh International and most of them use their own bathrooms or use the open place in front of jhuggis for bath. Data on place of bath (Table 6.6) shows that only 17.5 per cent of households take bath in the Sauchalayas and the rest (82.5 per cent) have their own arrangement. People do not use sauchalalya bathing facilities for several reasons. First, the Sauchalaya authority

TABLE 6.6 : PLACE FOR BATH

	Households	Percentage
Sulabh Sauchalaya	254	17.5
By own arrangement	1195	82.5
Total	1449	100

discourages the females taking bath because they claim that the females generally use more water for bathing and also washing clothes, which creates water shortage in the Sauchalayas. Secondly, Sauchalayas charge 0.50 paise per person, which the settlers consider to be on the higher side. Rather than spend money on this account, they make some kind of enclosure outside their jhugis and some even (generally females) take bath inside the jhuggi. In the latter case, males and children take bath in front of their houses.

Drainage System

The drainage system of the squatter settlement is extremely poor. This creates sanitary problem and storage of the sewage becomes breeding ground of diseases and also creates a filthy atmosphere with rancid smell. In the squatter settlement of the total 1449 household, 5 per cent households do not have any drainage at all (Table 6.7). Although the rest of the households have sewerage, 58 per cent have open drainage, and only 23.6 per cent of houses have covered drainage and the rest 13.4 per cent houses have other arrangements for sewage. Sewage in many places was found to be overflowing due to underground stagnation of sewage and absence of regular

TABLE 6.7 : DRAINAGE SYSTEM AROUND HOUSE

Type of Drainage	Households	Percentage
No drainage	73	5.0
Covered drainage	342	23.6
Open drainage	840	58.0
Others	194	13.4
Total	1449	100

cleaning. The safai karamcaris visit only once in a week which is not sufficient. Further, the sense of keeping the surroundings clean is very poor among the dwellers. Solid waste is dumped into the sewer blocking it.

Electricity

Among the squatter dwellers, 84.6 per cent households have electricity and the rest 15.4 per cent of households have no electricity (Table 6.8). Although more than three-fourths of the households have electricity, this is in the form of only one bulb in each household and the connection is not permanent. There is also danger of electrocution and sparking because of poor wire connections and above all, these connections are illegal.

TABLE 6.8 : AVAILABILITY OF ELECTRICITY

	Households	*Percentage*
Yes	1226	84.6
No	223	15.4
Total	1449	100.0

Type of Fuel

The type of fuel used for cooking is another indicator of the quality of life. Table 6.9, giving information regarding the type of fuel used for cooking, shows that most of the households (88.4 per cent) use kerosene as fuel. Of the rest, 1.4 per cent households use wood and 9.9 per cent households use both kerosene and wood as fuel for cooking. Only 0.4 per cent of households use cooking gas as fuel. Kerosene, being cheap and also available at the public distribution system, is used by most of the households. Wood, easily not available in this region and which also has high value, is used by lesser number of households. Those households which used wood generally collect it from their work-place, like gardeners working in district parks or a factory worker from the wooden packages or a shopkeeper of fruit and vegetables from the fruit packages. Gas, being the most expensive fuel, is used only by a small number of households.

TABLE 6.9 : COOKING FUEL

Fuel Type	*Households*	*Percentage*
Gas	6	0.4
Kerosene	1280	88.4
Wood	20	1.4
Kerosene and wood	143	9.9
Total	1449	100.0

Housing and Level of Living

In this section, we enquire whether the use and availability of basic amenities such as water, toilet, bathroom and electricity and use of fuel (gas, kerosene) and others varies according to type of house, namely pucca house, semi-pucca house and kutcha house. The availability of these amenities is cross-classified by the type of households and presented in Table 6.10

There are two sources of water supply in the squatter settlement, viz., tap and hand pump. Tap water points are available for public use while the hand pumps are mostly privately owned. It is observed that the hand pumps are available on a relatively higher scale in pucca house (16.71 per cent) and semi-pucca house (15.13 per cent) and least in kutcha house (13 per cent).

In case of toilet facility also (Table 6.10) the proportion of people using own toilet is more in case of pucca house (2.2 per cent) than the kutcha and semi-pucca houses.

In the case of toilet facility the proportion of households having their own arrangement is more in the case of semi-pucca house and pucca house, than kutcha house. Owners of semi-pucca house reported that they used some kind of enclosure made of Chataie or plastic for bathing in their households, for developing a bathroom of this type is much less costly than using a toilet.

Like toilet, the percentage of households having electricity connection is more in case of owners of pucca and semi-pucca house than kutcha house.

In case of gas for cooking, although a small number of household use it, the use was higher in case of pucca house

TABLE 6.10 : AMENITIES AVAILABLE IN KUTCHA, PUCCA AND SEMI-PUCCA HOUSES

	Type of House							
Amenity	*Kutcha*	*%*	*Pucca*	*%*	*Semi-pucca*	*%*	*Total*	*%*
Source of water								
Tap	663	86.61	264	83.28	314	84.86	1241	85.0
Handpump	99	13.00	53	16.71	56	15.13	208	14.0
	762	100 .00	317	100.00	370	100.00	1449	100.0
Place of toilet								
Public	754	99.00	310	97.80	367	99.19	1431	98.8
Private	8	1.00	7	2.20	3	0.81	18	1.2
	762	100.00	317	100.00	370	100.00	1449	100.0
Place of bathing								
Public	154	20.20	52	16.40	48	13.00	254	17.5
Private	608	79.80	265	83.60	322	87.00	1195	82.5
	762	100.00	317	100.00	370	100.00	1449	100.0
Electricity connection								
No	131	17.20	32	10.10	60	16.20	223	15.4
Yes	631	82.80	285	89.90	310	83.8	1226	84.6
	762	100.00	317	100.00	370	100.00	1449	100.00
Cooking fuel								
Gas	2	0.26	3	0.94	1	0.27	6	0.4
Kerosene	658	86.35	287	90.53	335	90.54	1280	88.4
Wood	15	1.97	1	0.31	4	1.08	20	1.4
Ker.+ Wood	87	11.42	26	8.20	30	8.10	143	9.9
	762	100.00	317	100.00	370	100.00	1449	100.0

owners, and less among the Semi-pucca house owners than kutcha house owners. Same is the case of the use of kerosene as fuel.

Thus virtually for all amenities, the pucca and semi-pucca house owner have a better access as compared to the kutcha house owners.

Health Facilities

Information on the use of public and private health services is given in Table 6.11. It shows that an equal number of households used health services from the private (34 per cent) and government (34 per cent) doctors for treatment and the

TABLE 6.11 : MODE OF TREATMENT

Agency of Treatment	*Households*	*Percentage*
Private	492	34.0
Government	491	33.9
Both	466	32.1
Total	1449	100

remaining 32 per cent used both private and government doctors. This indicates a relatively substantial number of poor families did not avail public health facilities for treatment and prefer to go to private doctors. The main reason for their preference (Table 6.12) is better treatment provided by them. In fact 91 per cent or the persons indicate better services as the main reason for treatment from the private doctor. The other reasons are, emergency (6.61 per cent), less time taken in private clinics (0.20 per cent), better infrastructure (0.52 per cent) and others (1.26 per cent). Although private doctors charge more, immediate and personalised attention compensates for their higher charges. Again the squatter dwellers require quick and easy access to a doctor, so that the loss of wage earning on a daily basis would be minimal.

TABLE 6.12 : REASONS FOR GOING TO PRIVATE DOCTORS

Reason	*Households*	*Percentage*
Emergency	63	6.61
Better treatment	871	91.40
Less time-consuming	2	0.20
Better facilities	5	0.53
Others	12	1.26
Total	953	100.00

Of those who prefer government doctors (Table 6.13) about 71.40 per cent households do so because of cheap treatment, 18.78 per cent due to free supply of medicine by the government dispensaries and 4.44 per cent due to emergency cases and 3.40 per cent due to serious diseases which if treated by private doctors, would cost more.

TABLE 6.13 : REASONS FOR GOING TO GOVERNMENT DOCTORS

Reason	*Households*	*Percentage*
Free medicine	182	18.78
Cheap treatment	695	71.72
Emergency cases	43	4.44
Serious diseases	33	3.40
Others	16	1.66
Total	969	100.00

Use of Ration card

Most households (97.9 per cent) possess ration cards (Table 6.14). Nevertheless they face several problems in availing the public distribution system. Irregular supply and lack of ration in the shops are the main problems the dwellers faced quite frequently. As a result, many of them have to resort to private shops. Information regarding purchase from outside is given in Table 6.15. It is seen from the table that only 0.41 per cent households get sufficient ration. More than half (51.24 per cent) of the households received up to 50 per cent ration, 27.90 per cent get 51–75 per cent ration, and 17.36 per cent get 76–94 per cent ration. Inadequate supply of ration results in purchase from outside. The results show that about 19 per cent of the households purchase one-fourth of the ration from outside. 63.02 per cent households purchase 26–50 percentage of the ration from outside. 12.32 per cent families purchase 51–75 percentage of the ration, 2.4 per cent families purcahse 76.99 per cent of the ration from outside.

TABLE 6.14 : POSSESSION OF RATION CARD

	Households	*Percentage*
Yes	1419	97.9
No	30	2.1
Total	1449	100

Among the causes which lead to purchase from outside (Table 6.16), irregular supply of ration (38.38 per cent) emerged

TABLE 6.15 : AVAILING OF RATION FACILITY

Percentage of Ration	*Purchasing from ration shop*	*%age*	*Purchasing from outside*	*%age*
Up to 25%	30	3.09	187	18.60
26% to 50%	496	51.24	634	63.02
51% to 75%	270	27.90	124	12.32
76% to 99%	168	17.36	24	2.39
100%	4	0.41	37	3.68
Total	968	100.00	1006	100.00

as the main cause. Non-availability of ration at the public distribution shop is another important reason (35.52 per cent). About 26.60 per cent households reported that the ration supplied in the distribution system does not meet their requirement.

TABLE 6.16 : REASONS FOR PURCHASE FROM OUTSIDE

Reason	*Households*	*Percentage*
Non-availability of ration	347	35.52
Irregular supply of ration	375	38.38
Not sufficient for family	255	26.10
Total	977	100.00

Distance of School

There is no school for the squatter dwellers except one balwadi centre, with the result that the children go outside the settlement for schooling. Information regarding distance of school is given in Table 6.17. It shows that 8.90 per cent of the children attend school or Balwadi located in the settlement.

Most of the children (67.95 per cent) attend the schools within a distance of 1 kilometre. About 17.20 per cent children have to travel a distance of 1 to 3 kilometres to attend school, nearly 7.18 per cent 3–5 kilometres, and only 0.57 per cent have to travel up to 5–7 kilometres. These are mostly the students going to higher secondary schools.

TABLE 6.17 : DISTANCE OF SCHOOL

School Distance	*No. of respondents*	*Percentage*
Within the settlement	78	8.90
Up to 1 km	596	67.95
1 km to 3 kms	125	14.25
3 kms to 5 kms	63	7.18
5 kms to 7 kms	5	0.57
More than 7 kms	10	1.14
Total	877	100.00

Recreation

Poverty and economic preoccupations do not permit the squatter settlement dwellers to have recreation. Spending the day's income on urban mode of entertainment (cinema, theatre, etc.) is near-impossible for them. Again, the fact that most of the people return home late in the evening after a day's work does not allow opportunities for leisure.

The only means of recreation left is listening to transistors and watching television either of their own or others. The celebration of festivals like Holi, Dusehra, Diwali and other religious festivals is the only occasion which provides collective recreation and community participation. Small temples and mosques constructed by inhabitants of the settlement provide the focus of social and religious gathering during religious occasions. Information about the recreation of the dwellers (Table 6.18) shows that 42.7 per cent of the households reported to have some recreation and the rest 57.3 per cent declined having any recreation. In the case of former, watching television is the most popular mode of recreation and this is mostly done by children and women.

TABLE 6.18 : RECREATION

	Households	*Percentage*
Yes	618	42.7
No	831	57.3
Total	1449	100.0

Visiting the library is not popular among the squatter dwellers. Only 1.1 per cent respondents reported having visited a library (Table 6.19).

TABLE 6.19 : VISITS TO LIBRARY

	Households	*Percentage*
Yes	16	1.1
No	1433	98.9
Total	1449	100.0

Summing up

The living environment of the squatter settlement is of poor quality. Its inhabitants are denied access to basic amenities and social services. Water supply to the squatter settlement is characterised by low pressure, less duration and uncertain flow in the summer months. Above all, a high pressure of 400 population is served by one tap. Although most households depend on Sulabh International for toilet facility with a minimal charge of 25 paise, the use density of around 130 people per one lavatory seat is very high. In the monsoon months, the dwellers face problems of using the Sauchalayas as half of the seats are choked. In the squatter settlement, only 18 households have their own toilet.

The dwellers face problems with regard to provision for bath. The high charge for taking bath and restriction on females bathing in the Sulabh creates problem. Some dwellers make some kind of enclosure outside their jhuggis to take bath and yet in some cases, females take bath inside their jhuggis.

Drainage system in the squatter is very poor. Overflow and stagnation of sewage are a common sight due to absence of regular cleaning and poor sense of cleanliness. Some houses are not even connected by sewerage and where they are connected most of the sewerage is open or uncovered.

More than half of the jhuggis are made of kutcha materials; another one-fourth are made of semi-pucca materials and only 21.9 per cent are made of pucca materials. Electricity connection to the jhuggis is not proper and permanent. Most families use kerosene fuel for cooking, around one-tenth of the households use both kerosene and wood for cooking. Only a small number of families use gas for cooking.

As regards access to health facilities a substantial number of families are not able to make use of government hospitals for treatment, preferring to go to private hospitals. Better treatment, immediate and personalised attention of the private doctors and unsympathetic attitude of the doctors and staff in government hospitals are the main reasons. Above all, the slum dwellers want quick and easy access to a doctor, so that they are able to minimize their loss of wage income due to ill health.

Although most households have a ration card, irregular supply and lack of ration at the distribution centre force them to purchase from the open market. Only 0.4 per cent households get sufficient ration and more than half households get only half of the ration.

Most of the school-going children travel up to a distance of about one kilometre. Some school-going children however have to travel for more than seven kilometres.

Poverty and busy occupational life do not permit the squatter settlement dwellers to spare time for recreation. The most popular means of recreation for them is listening to transistor and watching television, either their own or of others. Celebrations at religious festivals are the only occasion which provide collective recreation and community participation.

NOTES

1. T. Mathew, Economic Aspects of Housing, *Financial Express*, 30th December, 1987
2. Census of India, 1991, Housing and Amenities, Occasional paper No. 5, of 1994, Registrar General and Census Commissioner, India.

Chapter 7

Overview

With the growing urbanization of Delhi there has been a simultaneous expansion of slums as well, the number of slum settlements expanded by nearly twenty times between 1951 and 1991. The city has currently about 929 slum settlements. The present study was undertaken to examine the selected aspects of the social, economic and civic life of the slum population with focus on their demographic characteristics, migration pattern, occupation, income, infrastructure, civic amenities and others. The sample settlement named Bhumiheen camp located near Kalkaji DDA flats, situated five kilometres from Nehru Place in the south-eastern direction, surrounded by the New Okhla Industrial Development Area (NOIDA) was selected for the study. A sample of 1407 households with a total population of 5639 was drawn. The sample households were drawn from religious and caste groups also with the purpose of bringing out the differences between them with information on several aspects.

The study has tried to look into the relevant issues and questions which have been raised in a discussion on slum settlements. What are the demographic characteristics of the slum dwellers in terms of age composition, sex ratio, educational levels and others? Who are the migrants? Which region do they come from? Why do they migrate? What is their economic and social background (in terms of ownership of income-earning assets, caste and religion) at the place of origin? What are the sources of contact in migration? What are their present occupations and are these occupations different from those in the place of origin? Have they been able to change the occupation through acquiring education, skill or both? What is the level of income and of poverty? Finally, what is the quality of life in terms of access to housing, water, electricity, health facilities, public distribution system, recreation facilities and others? What follows are the main observations on these issues, which are analysed in greater detail in the preceding chapters, and also note their implications for policy and further research.

Demographic features

The squatter settlement under study is predominantly populated by the Hindus (88 per cent) followed by Muslim (10.21 per cent). Other religious groups such as Sikhs, Christians and Buddhists account for about one per cent of the sample population. The disparities in terms of caste composition are quite significant. The Scheduled Castes constitute nearly 56 per cent of the Hindu population (Hindus themselves accounting for 88 per cent of the total slum population). In fact Scheduled Castes (SC) account for nearly half the total population of the slum (i.e. including all religious groups and castes). Next come the Other Backward Classes (OBC) and higher castes in that order.

The sex ratio is generally lower than the Delhi average. It is particularly low among the Other Backward Classes (OBC) and Scheduled Tribes. The people's age composition indicates significant imbalances.

More than 40 per cent of the surveyed are below fifteen years of age and another 35 per cent are in the age group of 15 to 34 years. Thus the dependence on relatively young workers is quite high. The sex ratio and age composition seem to be greatly influenced by migration which in turn is influenced by economic considerations. While male migration is heavily induced by the search for employment, female migration is mainly due to marriage followed by employment.

As regards education close to 60 per cent of persons are literate but the literacy rate is lower among the Muslims and also somewhat lower among the Scheduled Castes and Scheduled Tribes than among high-caste persons. Most of the educated are concentrated in primary and middle-level education. A small proportion of them have reached higher education. This is particularly the case with the Scheduled Castes and Scheduled Tribes.

Of the total literates more than 95 per cent have education less than matriculation. As many as 45 per cent have education up to primary level. The population of those having education up to less than matriculate was slightly higher among the Muslims and OBCs. The need to take up employment in early life appears to be the main reason for the heavy drop-out among males.

Migration

About 86 per cent of migrants came from eastern India, namely Uttar Pradesh, Bihar, West Bengal and Bangladesh. The state of Uttar Pradesh alone accounts for 40 per cent of the migrants population in the slum. The rest of them are from Madhya Pradesh, Haryana, Rajasthan, Punjab, Orissa, Himachal Pradesh and Tamil Nadu. About 21 per cent of the migrants are from Bangladesh and Pakistan. The division of the subcontinent followed by war and riots are the main reasons for migration from these two regions. Employment, however, is the main reason for migration from the eastern states as nearly three-fourths of them indicated this specific reason for migration. Other reasons include family movement, marriage, flood, education and other. It is observed that about 56 per cent of the migration took place during the 1970s followed by the 1980s and some before 1970. The migration before 1970 was from Bangladesh and Pakistan and during the 1970s from the states of Uttar Pradesh, West Bengal, Bihar and Haryana during the 1980s migration was mainly from Orissa and Punjab. There seems to be a time dimension to migration. Migration during the 1970s was mainly induced by search for jobs, while before 1970 partition and riots caused most of it.

There is a significant age dimension to the flow of migration. Almost three-fourths of them migrated below the age of 25 years. Of this about 21 per cent was before 15 years of age and the remaining 45 per cent between 15 and 24 years of age. Beyond 35 years of age migration decreased, since the search for job, education and marriage generally gets reduced after the age of 35 years. However, migration on account of partition, riots or flood occurred irrespective of age.

It is also observed that part of the migration took place in stages. Although three-fourths of the migrants came directly to Delhi some of the migrants reached Delhi after having stayed at three or more places.

Distance seems to have a significant bearing on the stages in migration. Migrants from nearby states like Punjab, Haryana, Himachal Pradesh and Rajasthan migrated directly. Step-wise migration on the other hand was prominent among those coming from Bangladesh. Again, those who migrate do so more on account of contact. Contact with family numbers and relatives plays an important role in reaching this area. This is particularly the case of migration for employment, where connection and contact matter most. As regards the occupation pattern and job status, the overall level of Work Participation Rate (WPR) was about 31.52 per cent which was lower than the average WPR for urban Delhi.

WPR was even less for females than for male. Further, WPR tended to be lower among the low-income per capita households than among the relatively high-income groups indicating a positive relationship between WPR and monthly per capita income, which also means that relatively poor families have lesser employment opportunities.

The occupational pattern is fairly diversified and complex. Given the lower educational level and skill they are concentrated in manual and unskilled jobs. The occupations in which most of them are engaged include casual work in construction, factory worker, shopkeepers and vendors, tailors, maid-servant and other minor occupations. These occupations account for about 60 per cent of the total jobs. There are four industrial categories in which about three-fourths of the workers are engaged. These include construction (19.13 per cent), community, social and personal services (19.25 per cent) wholesale and retail trade (18.35 per cent) and manufacturing and repair (17.44 per cent). Generally more workers are engaged in the tertiary sector, followed by the secondary and primary sectors.

Looking at the occupational pattern from the employment status points of view, half of the workers are casual labour followed by one-third in petty self-employed activities and remaining one-fifth in regular salaried jobs. A relatively high proportion of Hindu workers are casual labour, with a high incidence of casual labour among the scheduled castes/ Scheduled Tribes. In fact Scheduled Caste workers account for nearly 61 per cent of the total casual worker, a ratio which is much higher than their share in the slum population and among workers. The Muslims are more in petty self-employed activities. In the regular salaried jobs the proportion of Hindus was higher, most of them from Other Backward Classes (OBC) and higher castes than Scheduled Tribes and Scheduled Castes.

We have also tried to see whether any change has occurred in the nature of occupation of their origin. There has been obviously change in the occupation but in terms of status it is not qualitatively and significantly different from the occupation of their origin. It is either mainly manual or semi-skilled in nature. While some workers who were manual labour at the place of origin have remained casual manual labour, others have switched over to factory work, shops, tailoring, printing and maid-servant. A similar shift is observed among those who were marginal/small farmers at the place of origin. Even among those who used to carry on traditional occupations like washerman, fisherman, goldsmith, blacksmith, barber have switched over to other occupations. As to carpenters and tailors, about half of them have retained their traditional occupation of origin.

Has migration brought about a significant change in the people's economic situation? The classification of the slum population according to monthly per capita consumption indicates that the monthly per capita income of 60 per cent of the households was less than Rs 309. To the extent income determines consumption level it can be said that about 66 per cent of the slum household population were below the poverty line (which is 309 HPCE for Delhi) in 1993–94. This is indeed a very high level of economic deprivation among the slum dwellers studied.

The situation regarding basic and civic amenities is not satisfactory either. The water supply is inadequate and uncertain with one tap available per four hundred persons. Similarly the dependence on lavatory seat is 130 persons per one lavatory. Out of the 1407 households only 14 have their own toilet facility. Similarly both public and private facilities for bath are extremely poor. Drainage system on the squatter is very poor. Overflow and stagnation of sewage is a common problem. Several sewerages are open or uncovered. As regards housing, more than half the jhuggis are made of kutcha material and another one-fourth are of semi-pucca material. The electricity connection in the jhuggis is not safe and permanent. In the case of health facilities, a substantial number of families are not able to make use of public hospitals. Further, although most households have a ration card, the lack of ration and its irregular supply force the dwellers to make purchases from the open market.

The results throw up important implications for urban policy with regard to physical development of slum settlement in the Metropolis and also the people living their in. It is clear that migration to the slum is essentially of push type. Most of migrants were either landless labour, marginal farmers or artisans at the place of their origin, who could not find adequate employment for minimum living. Most of them therefore migrated to the city in search of job. The fact that three-fourth of migrants are below the age of 25 years (21% below 15 years of the age and remaining 45% in the age group of 15 to 24 years), it is a clear indication of the distress situation and economic compulsions associated with push migration of the persons to the slum. Further, about 60% are literate and remaining 40% illiterate. Even among the literates, most of them are educated upto either primary or middle level. With such an intense economic compulsion and low level of education and skill, eventually somehow most of the migrants get absorbed in the urban labour market in categories of jobs, (such as casual work in construction, factory, shop keepers, vendors, tailors, maid servants etc.) which are manual or semi-skilled (involving traditional skill) in nature. Since there is not much improvement in the education and skill of the migrants, the new jobs in the city are not qualitively different from occupations of their origin. Even half of the artisans maintained their traditional occupation of origin. The earnings are less, variable and uncertain and hence the level of poverty among them is high. The quality of life in terms of civic aminities and housing is also quite low.

In this kind of situation, there are spheres where positive intervention by the state could help the people in the slum in a significant manner. The proper state intervention through the slum development authority is necessary at least in a few areas. First, since the literacy level and skill formation among the young workers is low, they have to mainly depend on the manual and semi-skilled jobs. It is here that the youth could be provided with various kinds of vocational training keeping in view the emerging labour market demand. At present, there is no such programme for the youth in the slum area, at least non of them seems to have gained access to vocational training.

Secondly, the migrants are able to get some kind of jobs on their own and work out a minimum level of living. But when it comes to civic aminities (such a water, electricity, sanitation and housing), the migrants live in sub-human environment. This is particularly true about the housing and sanitation. The urban land market is highly imperfect and beyond the reach of the people in the slum. The state should ensure that, reasonable housing and civic services are provided to the people who can not afford them due to distortion in the urban land market. Thirdly, the intervention and an appropriate support in sphere of public health services, supply of food through PDS and education is also called for. It is surprising that a substantial number of families were unable to take advantage of public hospital and PDS and therefore they had to resort to private health services and also to open market for food requirement presumably due to lack of public hospitals and schools in the vicinity. This is another area where state government's positive intervention would make a significant difference in the civic life of slum people.

ANNEXTURE I
HOUSEHOLD SCHEDULE

Part I : Demographic & Socio-Cultural

Serial No. : .... Religion : .... Caste: ....

Language: .... Name of slum: ....

Address: ....

....

House No.: ....

Whether the Household owns a ration card: ....

S.No.	*Household*	*Age*	*Sex*	*Relationship with head*	*Marital Status*				*Education*				*Reasons for leaving education*	*Remarks*
					M	*U*	*D*	*O*	*I*	*L*	*No. of years studied*	*Name of degree, diploma obtained*		

Note: 1. Mention if SC/ST

2. Marital status— M: married, U: unmarried, W: widowed, D: divorced, O: other

3. Education—I: illiterate, L: literate.

Part II : Migration History

S.No.

Name of migrant ....

Age at migration ....

Sex ....

Purpose of migration ....

Place of origin ....

When did you leave your home town/village first ....

How many places did you stay at before moving to Delhi? ....

Since when are you in Delhi? ....

Occupation at place of origin ....

Your contact in migration to Delhi ....

Note: Purpose of migration—education, employment, marriage, family moved, others (specify).

Place of origin—Give the name of town/village, district, state

Place of stay—Write down the name of the places/states.

Occupation at place of origin—LL: landless labour; LO: landowner, give also the land owned; O: others, specify the occupation.

Part III : Economic Activities

Member in Household:	Total	M	F
Workers:	Total	M	F
Non-workers:	Total	M	F

S.No.

Household members ....

Age ....

Sex ....

Educational level ....

Employment status ....

Employer & place ....

Nature of work ....

Full-time/part-time ....

Duration of employment (days in): .... a week .... month ...... year

Monthly income (Rs.)...

Place of work Name Distance

....

....

Note: Educational level—I: illiterate; L: literate and no. of years of schooling; any specific course completed, and name of the course

Employment status: Self-employment/employee/any other

Household Schedule

Part IV : Infrastructure: Housing and Other Facilities

S.No.

TENURE STATUS OF HOUSE

Building material used: Roof................ Wall............ Floor..............

Source of water: ....

Location of water facility: ....

Electricity: ....

Place for bath: ....

Kitchen: ....

Drain line: ....

Fuel as source of cooking:...

Remarks: ....

....

Note: Tenure status of house—owned/rented/any other (specify).

Source of water—tap/handpump/well/municipal tap/any other (specify)

Location of water facility—inside the premises/outside the premises; if outside also mention approx. distance

Electricity—internal connecton/outside connection; if outside mention approx. distance

Toilet and bath—where located; if outside, distance.

Kitchen—inside the premises/outside; if outside, where

Access to Civic Facilities and Amenities

1. Health

i) Where do you go for medical treatment?

ii) If going to private doctor, why?

iii) If going to government hospital, why?

2. Food Supply

i) Do you have a ration card?

ii) Do you purchase your full entitlement?

iii) If not, how much from ration shop, how much from outside?

3. Education

i) Where do your children go for school?

ii) At what level?

iii) How far is the school/college from house?

iv) Do you attend adult education classes?

4. Recreation

i) Where do you go for a movie or any other recration?

ii) Do yo go to library? If yes, where?

5. Banks and finance

i) Have you ever taken loan from Bank?

ii) If yes, purpose for which loan was taken?

iii) How far is the bank?

ANNEXURE II

THE SLUM AREAS (IMPROVEMENT AND CLEARANCE) ACT, 1956

(96 of 1956)

[29th December, 1956]

An Act to provide for the improvement and clearance of slum areas in certain Union territories and for the protection of tenants in such areas from eviction.

Be it enacted by the Parliament in the seventh year of the Republic of India as follows:—

CHAPTER I
PRELIMINARY

1. Short title, extent and commencement.—(1) This Act may be called the Slum Area (Improvement and Clearance) Act, 1956.

(2) It extends to all Union territories except the Union territories of the Andaman and Nicobar Islands and the Laccadive, Minicoy and Amindivi Islands.*

(3) It shall come into force in a Union territory on such date[1] as the Central Government may, by notification in the Official Gazette, appoint; and different dates may be appointed for different Union territories.

2. Definitions.—In this Act unless the context otherwise requires,—

(a) "Administrator" means the Administrator of a Union territory;

(b) "building" includes any structure or erection or any part of a building as so defined but does not include plant or machinery comprised in a building;

---

1. Came into force in the Union territory of Delhi on the 8th February, 1957, *vide* S.R.O. 421, dated 4th February, 1957, published in the Gazette of India, Pt. II, Sec. 3, p. 256 and in the Union territory of Tripura on 1st April, 1958, *vide* S.O. 414, dated 31st March, 1958, published in the Gazette of India, Pt. II, Sec. 30(ii), p.256.
Extended to Pondicherry by Act 26 of1968, Sec. 4 and Sch.

* Islands were renamed as Lakshadweep in 1973

(c) "competent authority" means such officer or authority as the Administrator may, be notification in the Official Gazette, appoint as the competent authority for the purpose of this Act;

(d) "erection" in relation to a building includes extension, alteration or re-erection;

[1][(e) "land" includes benefits to arise out of land, and things attached to the earth or permanently fastened to anything attached to the earth;

(f) "occupier" includes—

(a) any person who for the time being is paying or is liable to pay to the owner the rent or any portion of the rent of the land or building in respect of which such rent is paid or is payable;

(b) an owner in occupation of, or otherwise using his land or building;

(c) a rent-free tenant of any land or building;

(d) a licensee in occupation of any land or building; and

(e) any person who is liable to pay to the owner damages for the use and occupation of any land or building;]

(g) "owner" includes any person who is receiving or is entitled to receive the rent of any building or land whether on his own account or on behalf of himself and others or as agent or trustee, or who would so receive the rent or be entitled to receive it if the building or land were let to a tenant;

(h) "prescribed" means prescribed by rules made under this Act;

(i) "slum clearance" means the clearance of any slum area by the demolition and removal of buildings therefrom; and

[2][(j) "work of improvement" includes in relation to any building in a slum area the execution of any one or more of the following works, namely:—

(i) necessary repairs;

---

1. Subs. by Act No. 43 of 1964, Sec. 2, for clauses (e) and (f) (w.e.f. 27-2-1965).
2. Ins. by Act No. 43 of 1964, Sec. 2 (w.e.f. 27-2-1965).

(ii) structural alterations;
(iii) provision of light points, water taps and bathing places;
(iv) construction of drains, open or covered;
(v) provision of latrines, including conversion of dry latrines into water borne latrines;
(vi) provision of additional or improved fixtures or fittings;
(vii) opening up or paving of courtyards;
(viii) removal of rubbish; and
(ix) any other work including the demolition of any building or any part thereof which in the opinion of the competent authority is necessary for executing any of the works specified above.]

CHAPTER II
SLUM AREAS

3. Declaration of slum areas.—(1) Where the competent authority upon report from any of its officers or other information in its possession is satisfied as respects any area that the buildings in that area—

(a) are in any respect unfit for human habitation; or
(b) are by reason of dilapidation, overcrowding, faulty arrangement and design of such buildings, narrowness or faulty arrangement of streets, lack of ventilation, light or sanitation facilities, or any combination of these factors, are detrimental to safety, health or morals.

it may, by notification in the Official Gazette, declare such area to be a slum area.

(2) In determining whether a building is unfit for human habitation for the purposes of this Act, regard shall be had to its condition in respect of the following matters, that is to say—

(a) repair;
(b) stability;
(c) freedom from damp;
(d) natural light and air;
(e) water supply;
(f) drainage and sanitary conveniences;
(g) facilities for storage, preparation and cooking of food and for the disposal of waste water;

and the building shall be deemed to be unfit as aforesaid if and only if it is so far defective in one or more of the said matters that it is not reasonably suitable for occupation in that condition.

CHAPTER III
SLUM IMPROVEMENT

4. Power of competent authority to require improvement of buildings unfit for human habitation.— (1) Where the competent authority upon report from any of its officers or other information in its possession is satisfied that any building in a slum area is in any respect unfit for human habitation, it may, unless in its opinion the building is not capable at a reasonable expense of being rendered so fit, serve upon the owner of the building a notice requiring him within such time not being less than thirty days as may be specified in the notice to execute the works of improvement specified therein and stating that in the opinion of the authority those works will render the building fit for human habitation:

[1][Provided that where the owner of the building is different from the owner of the land on which the building stands and the works of improvement required to be executed relate to provision of water taps, bathing places, construction of drains, open or covered, as the case may be, provision of water-borne latrines or removal of rubbish and such works are to be executed outside the building, the notice shall be served upon the owner of the land.]

(2) In addition to serving a notice under this section on the owner the competent authority may serve a copy of the notice on any other person having an interest in the building [2][or the land on which the building stands] whether as lessee, mortgagee or otherwise.

(3) Indetermining, for the purposes of this Act, whether a building can be rendered fit for human habitation at a reasonable expense, regard shall be had to the estimated cost of the works necessary to render it so fit and the value which

---

1. Added by Act No. 43 of 1964, Sec. 3 (w.e.f. 27-2-1965).
2. Ins. by Act No. 43 of 1964, Sec. 3 (w.e.f. 27-2-1965).

it is estimated that the building will have when the works are completed.

5. Enforcement of notice requiring execution of works of improvement.—(1) If a notice under Section 4 requiring the owner of the building[1] [or of the land on which the building stands, as the case may be], to execute works of improvement is not complied with, then, after the expiration of the time specified in the notice the competent authority may itself do the works required to be done by the notice.

(2) All expenses incurred by the competent authority under this section, together with interest, at such rate as the Central Government may by order fix, from the date when a demand for the expenses is made until payment, may be recovered by the competent authority from the owner of the building [1][for of the land on which the building stands, as the case may be], as arrears of land revenue:

Provided that if the owner proves that he—

(a) is receiving the rent merely as agent or trustee for some other person; and

(b) has not in his hands on behalf of that other person sufficient money to satisfy the whole demand of the authority,

his liability shall be limited to the total amount of money which he has in his lands as aforesaid.

[2][***]

6. Expenses of maintenance of works of improvement etc., to be recoverable from the occupiers of buildings.— Where works of improvement have been executed in relation to any building in a slum area in pursuance of the provisions of sections 4 and 5, the expenses incurred by the competent authority or, as the case works may be, any local authority in connection with the maintenance of such works of improvement or the enjoyment of amenities and conveniences rendered possible by such works shall be recoverable from the occupier or occupiers of the building as arrears of land revenue.

[3][**6A. Restriction on buildings, etc., in slum areas.**—(1) The competent authority may, by notification in the Official

1. Ins. by Act No. 43 of 1964, Sec. 4 (w.e.f. 27-2-1965).
2. Sub-section (3) omitted by Act No. 43 of 1964, Sec. 4 (w.e.f. 27-2-1965).
3. Ins. by Act No. 43 of 1964, Sec. 5 (w.e.f. 27-2-1965).

Gazette, direct that no person shall erect any building in a slum area except with the previous permission in writing of the competent authority.

(2) Every notification issued under sub-section (1) shall cease to have effect on the expiration of two years from the date thereof except as respects things done or omitted be done before such cesser.

(3) Every person desiring to obtain the permission referred to in sub-section (1) shall give an application in writing to the competent authority in such form and containing such information in respect of the erection of the building to which the application relates as may be prescribed.

(4) On receipt of such application, the competent authority, after making such inquiry as it considers necessary, shall, by order in writing,—

(a) either grant the permission subject to such terms and conditions, if any, as may be specified in the order; or

(b) refuse to grant such permission:

Provided that before making an order refusing such permission, the applicant shall be given a reasonable opportunity to show cause why the permission should not be refused.

(5) Nothing contained in sub-section (1) shall apply to—

(a) any works of improvement required to be executed by a notice under sub-section (1) of section 4 or in pursuance of an undertaking given under sub-section (2) of section 7; or

(b) the erection of any building in any area in respect of which a slum clearance order has been made under section 10.]

7. Power of competent authority to order demolition of buildings unfit for human habitation.—(1) Where a competent authority upon a report from any of its officers or other information in its possession is satisfied that any building within a slum area is unfit for human habitation and is not capable at a reasonable expense of being rendered so fit, it shall serve upon the owner of the building, and upon any other person having an interest in the building, whether as lessee, mortgagee or otherwise, a notice to show cause within such time as may be specified in the notice as to why an order of demolition of the building should not be made.

(2) If any of the persons upon whom a notice has been served under sub-section (1), appears a pursuance thereof before the competent authority and gives an undertaking to the authority that such person shall within a period specified by the authority execute such works of improvement in relation to the building as well in the opinion of the authority render the building fit for human habitation, or that it shall not be used for human habitation until the authority on being satisfied that it has been rendered fit for that purpose cancels the undertaking, the authority shall not make any order of demolition of the building.

(3) It no such undertaking as is mentioned in sub-section (2) is given, or if in a case where any such undertaking has been given any work of improvement to which the undertaking relates is not carried out within the specified period, or building is at any time used in contravention of the terms of the undertaking, the competent authority shall forthwith make an order of demolition of the building requiring that the building shall be vacated within a period to be specified in the order not being less than thirty days from the date of the order, and that it shall be demolished within six weeks after the expiration of that period.

8. Procedure to be followed where demolition order has been made.—(1) Where an order for demolition of a building under section 7 has been made the owner of the building or any other person having an interest therein shall demolish that building within the time specified in that behalf by the order; and if the building is not demolished within that time the competent authority shall enter and demolish the building and sell the materials, thereof.

(2) Any expenses incurred by the competent authority under sub-section (1), if not satisfied out of the proceeds of sale of materials of the building shall be recoverable from the owner of the building or any other person having in interest therein as arrears of land revenue.

CHAPTER IV
SLUM CLEARANCE AND RE-DEVELOPMENT

9. Power to declare any slum area to be a clearance area.—(1) Where the competent authority upon a report from any of its officers or other information in its possession is satisfied as respects any slum area that the most satisfactory method of dealing with the conditions in the area is the demolition of all the buildings in the area, the authority shall by an order notified in the Official Gazette declare the area to be a clearance area, that is to say, an area to be cleared of all buildings in accordance with the provisions of this Act:

Provided that any building in the area which is not unfit for human habitation or dangerous or injurious to health may be excluded from the declaration if the authority considers it necessary.

(2) The competent authority shall forthwith transit to the Administrator a copy of the declaration under this section together with a statement of the number of persons who on a date specified in the statement were occupying buildings comprised in the clearance area.

10. Slum clearance order.—(1) As soon as may be after the competent authority has declared any slum area to be a clearance area, it shall make a slum clearance order in relation to that area ordering the demolition of each of the buildings specified therein and requiring each such building to be vacated within such time as may be specified in the order and submit the order to the Administrator for confirmation.

(2) The Administrator may either confirm the order *in toto* or subject to such variations as he considers necessary or reject the order.

(3) If the Administrator confirms the order, the order shall become operative from the date of such confirmation.

(4) When a slum clearance order has become operative, the owners of buildings to which the order applies shall demolish the buildings before the expiration of six weeks from the date on which the buildings are required by the order to be vacated or before the expiration of such longer period as in the circumstances of the case the competent authority may deem reasonable.

(5) If the buildings are not demolished before the expiration of the period mentioned in sub-section (4), the competent authority shall enter and demolish the buildings and sell the materials thereof.

(6) Any expenses incurred by the competent authority in

demolishing any building shall, if not satisfied out of the proceeds of sale of materials thereof, be recoverable by the competent authority as arrears of land revenue.

[1][(7) Subject to the provisions of this Act, where a slum clearance order has become operative, the owner of the land to which the order applies may re-develop the land in accordance with plans approved by the competent authority and subject to such restrictions and conditions (including a condition with regard to the time within which the re-development shall be completed), if any, as that authority may think fit to impose:

Provided that an owner who is aggrieved by a restriction or condition so imposed on the user of his land or by a subsequent refusal of the competent authority to cancel or modify such restriction or condition may, within such time as may be prescribed, appeal to the Administrator and the Administrator shall make such order in the matter as he thinks proper and his decision shall be final.]

(8) No person shall commence or cause to be commenced any work in contravention of a plan approved or a restriction or condition imposed under sub-section (7).

[2][**11. Power of competent authority to re-develop clearance area.**—(1) Notwithstanding anything contained in sub-section (7) of section 10, the competent authority may at any time after the land has been cleared of the buildings in accordance with a slum clearance order but before the work of re-development of that land has been commenced by the owner by order, determine to re-develop the land if that authority is satisfied that it is necessary in the public interest to do so.

(2) Where land has been cleared of the buildings in accordance with a slum clearance order, the competent authority, if it is satisfied that the land has been, or is being re-developed by the owner thereof in contravention of plans approved by the authority or any restrictions or conditions imposed under sub-section (7) of section 10 or has not been redeveloped within the time, if any, specified under such conditions, may by order, determine to re-develop the land:

Provided that before passing such order, the owner shall be

1. Sub. by Act No. 43 of 1964, Sec. 6 (w.e.f. 27-2-1965).
2. Sub. by Act No. 43 of 1964, Sec. 7, for section 11 (w.e.f. 27-2-1965).

given a reasonable opportunity to show cause why the order should not be passed.]

CHAPTER V
ACQUISITION OF LAND

12. Power of the Central Government to acquire land.—(1) Where on any representation from the competent authority it appears to the Central Government that, in order to enable the authority to execute any work of improvement in relation to any building in a slum area or to re-develop any clearance area, it is necessary that land within, adjoining or surrounded by any such area should be acquired, the Central Government may acquire the land by publishing in the Official Gazette a notice to the effect that the Central Government has decided to acquire the land in pursuance of this section:

Provided that before publishing such notice, the Central Government may call upon the owner of, or any other person who, in the opinion of the Central Government, may be interested in, such land to show cause why it should not be acquired; and after considering the cause, if any shown by the owner or any other person interested in the land, the Central Government may pass such order as it deems fit.

(2) When a notice as aforesaid is published in the Official Gazette, the land shall on and from the date on which the notice is so published, vest absolutely in the Central Government free from the all encumbrances.

13. Land acquired by Central Government to be made available to the competent authority.—Where any land in a slum area or clearance area has been acquired under this Act the Central Government shall make the land available to the competent authority for the purpose of executing any work of improvement or carrying out any order of demolition or for the purpose of re-development:

[1][Provided that where on any representation from the competent authority, the Central Government is satisfied that any such land or any portion thereof is unsuitable for the purpose mentioned in this section, the Central Government

1. Added by Act No. 43 of 1964, Sec. 8 (w.e.f. 27-2-1965).

may use the land or allow it to be used for such other public purpose or purposes as it may deem fit.]

14. Right to receive compensation.—Every person having any interest in any land acquired under this Act shall be entitled to receive from the Central Government compensation as provided hereafter in this Act.

15. Basis for determination of compensation.—(1) The amount payable as compensation in respect of any land acquired under this Act shall be an amount equal to sixty times the net average monthly income actually derived from such land during the period of five consecutive years immediately preceding the date of publication of the notice referred to in section 12.

(2) The net average monthly income referred to in sub-section (1) shall be calculated in the manner and in accordance with the principles set in the Schedule.

(3) The competent authority shall, after holding an inquiry in the prescribed manner determine in accordance with the provisions of sub-section (2) the net average monthly income actually derived from the land and publish a notice in the Official Gazette specifying the amount so determined and calling upon the owner of the land and every person interested therein to intimate to it before a date specified in the notice whether such owner or person agrees to the amount so determined and if he does not so agree, what amount he claims to be the net average monthly income actually derived from the land.

(4) Any person who does not agree to the amount of the net average monthly income determined by the competent authority under sub-section (3) and claims a sum in excess of that amount may prefer an appeal to the Administrator within thirty days from the date specified in the notice referred to in that sub-section.

(5) On appeal the Administrator shall, after hearing the appellant, determine the net average monthly income and his determination shall be final and shall not be questioned in any court of law.

(6) Where there is any building on the land in respect of which the net average monthly income has been determined, no separate compensation shall be paid in respect of such building:

Provided that where the owner of the land and the owner of the building on such land are different, the competent authority shall apportion the amount of compensation between the owner of the land and the owner of the building [1][in the same proportion as the market price of land bears to the market price of the building on the date of the acquisition].

[2][* * *]

16. Apportionment of compensation.—(1) Where several persons claim to be interested in the amount of compensation determined under section 15, the competent authority shall determine the persons who in its opinion are entitled to receive compensation and the amount payable to each of them.

(2) If any dispute arises as to the apportionment of compensation or any part thereof, or as to the persons to whom the same or any part thereof is payable, the Competent Authority may refer the dispute to the decision of the Administrator; and the Administrator in deciding any such dispute shall follow, as far as may be, the provisions of Part III of the Land Acquisition Act, 1894 (1 of 1894).

17. Payment of compensation or deposit of the same in court.—(1) After the amount of compensation has been determined, the competent authority shall on behalf of the Central Government tender payment of, and pay, the compensation to the persons entitled thereto.

(2) If the persons entitled to compensation do not consent to receive it, or if there be any dispute as to the title to receive compensation or as to the apportionment of it, the competent authority shall deposit the amount of the compensation in the court of the District Judge and that court shall deal with the amount so deposited in the manner laid down in sections 32 and 33 of the Land Acquisition Act, 1894 (1 of 1894).

18. Powers of competent authority in relation to determination of compensation, etc.—(1) The competent authority may, for the purposes of determining the amount of the compensation or apportionment thereof, require, by order, any person to furnish such information in his possession as may be specified in the order.

1. Sub. by Act No. 43 of 1964, Sec. 9 for "in such proportion as he considers reasonable" (w.e.f. 27-2-1965).
2. Second proviso omitted by Act No. 43 of 1964, Sec. 9 (w.e.f. 27-2-1965).

(2) The competent authority shall, while holding inquiry under section 15, have all the powers of a civil court while trying a suit under the Code of Civil Procedure, 1908 (5 of 1908), in respect of the following matters, namely:—

(a) summoning and enforcing the attendance of any person and examining him on oath;

(b) requiring the discovery and production of any document;

(c) reception of evidence on affidavits;

(d) requisitioning any public record from any court or office;

(e) issuing commissions for examination of witnesses.

CHAPTER VI
PROTECTION OF TENANTS IN SLUM AREAS FROM EVICTION

[1][**19. Proceedings for eviction of tenants not to be taken without permission of the competent authority.**— (1) Notwithstanding anything contained in any other law for the time being in force, no person shall, except with the previous permission in writing of the competent authority.—

(a) institute, after the commencement of the Slum Areas (Improvement and Clearance), Amendment Act, 1964 any suit or proceeding for obtaining any decree or order for the eviction of a tenant from any building or land in slum area; or

(b) where any decree or order is obtained in any suit or proceeding instituted before such commencement for the eviction of a tenant from any building or land in such area, execute such decree or order.

(2) Every person desiring to obtain the permission referred to in sub-section (1) shall make an application in writing to the competent authority in such form and containing such particulars as may be prescribed.

(3) On receipt of such application, the competent authority, after giving an opportunity to the parties of being heard and after making such summary inquiry into the circumstances of the case as it thinks fit, shall by order in writing, either grant or refuse to grant such permission.

(4) In granting or refusing to grant the permission under

---

1. Sub. by Act No. 43 of 1964, Sec. 10, for Sec. 19 (w.e.f. 27-2-1965).

sub-section (3), the competent authority shall take into account the following factors, namely:—

(a) whether alternative accommodation within the means of the tenant would be available to him if he were evicted;

(b) whether the eviction is in the interest of improvement and clearance of the slum areas;

(c) such other factors, if any, as may be prescribed.

(5) Where the competent authority refuses to grant the permission, it shall record a brief statement of the reasons for such refusal and furnish a copy thereof to the applicant.]

[1][**20. Appeals.**—Any person aggrieved by an order of the competent authority refusing to grant the permission referred to in sub-section (1) of section 6A or referred to in sub-section (1) of section 19 may, within such time as may be prescribed, prefer an appeal to the Administrator and the Administrator may, after hearing the appellant, decide such appeal and his decision shall be final.

[2][**20A. Restoration of possession of premises vacated by a tenant.**—(1) Where a tenant in occupation of any building in a slum area vacates any building or is evicted therefrom on the ground that it was required for the purpose of executing any work of improvement or for the purpose of re-erection of the building, the tenant may, within such time as may be prescribed, file a declaration with the competent authority that he desires to be replaced in occupation of the building after the completion of the work of improvement or re-erection of the building as the case may be.

(2) On receipt of such declaration, the competent authority shall by order require the owner of the building to furnish to it, within such time as may be prescribed, the plans of the work of improvement or re-erection of the building and estimates of the cost thereof and such other particulars as may be necessary and shall, on the basis of such plans and estimates and particulars, if any, furnished and having regard to the provisions of sub-section (3) of section 20B and after holding such inquiry as it may think fit, provisionally determine

1. Sub. by Act No. 43 of 1964, Sec. 11, for Sec. 19 (w.e.f. 27-2-1965).
2. Ins. by Act No. 43 of 1964, Sec. 12, (w.e.f. 27-2-1965).

the rent that would be payable by the tenant if he were to be replaced in occupation of the building in pursuance of the declaration made by him under sub-section (1).

(3) The rent provisionally determined under sub-section (2) shall be communicated in the prescribed manner to the tenant and the owner.

(4) If the tenant after the receipt of such communication intimates in writing to the competent authority within such time as may be prescribed that when he is replaced in occupation of the building in pursuance of the declaration made by him under sub-section (1), he would pay to the owner until the rent is finally determined under section 20B the rent provisionally determined under sub-section (2), the competent authority shall direct the owner to place the tenant in occupation of the building after the completion of the work of improvement of re-erection of the building, as the case may be, and the owner shall be bound to comply with such direction.

20B. Rent of buildings in slum areas.—(1) Where any building in a slum area is let to a tenant after the execution of any work of improvement or after it has been re-erected, the rent of the building shall be determined in accordance with the provisions of this section.

(2) Where any such building is let to a tenant other than a tenant who is placed in possession of the building in pursuance of a direction issued under sub-section (4) of section 20A, the tenant shall be liable to pay to the owner—

(a) if there is a general law relating to the control of rents in force in the area in which the building is situated and applicable to that building, the rent determined in accordance with the provisions of that law;

(b) if there is no such law in force in such area, such rent as may be agreed upon between the owner and the tenant.

(3) Where any such building is let to a tenant in pursuance of a direction issued under sub-section (4) of section 20A, the tenant shall, notwithstanding any law relating to the control of rents in force in the area, be liable to pay to the owner—

(a) If any work of improvement has been executed in relation to the building, an annual rent of a slum equivalent to the aggregate of the following amounts, namely:—

(i) the annual rent the tenant was paying immediately before he vacated the building for the purpose of execution of the work of improvement;

(ii) six per cent of the cost of the work of improvement; and

(iii) six per cent of a sum equivalent of the compensation payable in respect of any land which may have been acquired for the purpose of effecting such improvement as if such land were acquired under section 12 on the date of the commencement of the work of improvement.

(b) if the building has been re-erected, an annual rent of a sum equivalent to four per cent of the aggregate cost of reconstruction of the building and the cost of the land on which the building is re-erected.

Explanation—For the purposes of this clause, the cost of the land shall be deemed to be a sum equivalent to the compensation payable in respect of the land if it were acquired under section 12 on the date of the commencement of the reconstruction of the building.

(4) The rent payable by a tenant in respect of any building under sub-section (3) shall, on an application made by the tenant or the owner, be determined by the authority referred in sub-section (5):

Provided that an application for determination of such rent by the owner or the tenant shall not, except for sufficient cause, be entertained by such authority after the expiry of ninety days from the completion of the work of improvement or re-erection of the building, as the case may be.

(5) The authority to which the application referred to in sub-section (4) shall be made, shall be—

(a) where there is a general law relating to the control of rents in force in the area in which the building is situate, the authority to whom applications may be made for fixing of rents of buildings situate in that area, and for the purpose of determining the area under this section that authority may exercise all or any of the powers it has under the said general law, and the provisions of such law including provisions relating to appeals shall apply accordingly.

(b) if there is of such law in force in that area, such authority as may be specified by rules made in this behalf by the Central Government and such rules may provide the procedure that will be followed by that authority in determining the rent and also for appeals against the decision of such authority.

(6) Where the rent is finally determined under this section, then the amount of rent paid by the tenant shall be adjusted against the rent so finally determined and if the amount so paid falls short of, or is in excess of, the rent finally determined, the tenant shall pay the deficiency or entitled to a refund, as the case may be.]

21. Chapter not to apply to eviction of tenants from certain buildings.—Nothing in this Chapter shall apply to or in relation to the [1][eviction under any law] of a tenant from any building in a slum area belonging to the Government, [2][the Delhi Development authority] or any local authority.

CHAPTER VII
MISCELLANEOUS

22. Powers of entry.—In shall be lawful for any purpose authorised by the competent authority in this behalf to enter into or upon any building or land in a slum area with or without assistants or workmen in order to make any inquiry, inspection, measurement, valuation or survey, or to execute any work which is authorised by or under this Act or which it is necessary to execute for any of the purposes or in pursuance of any of the provisions of this Act or of any rule or order made thereunder.

23. Powers of inspection.—(1) The competent authority may, by general or special order, authorise any person—

(a) to inspect any drain, latrine, urinal, cesspool, pipe, sewer or channel in or on any building or land in a slum area, and in this discretion to cause the ground to be opened for the purpose of preventing or removing any nuisance arising from the drain, latrine, urinal, cesspool, pipe, sewer or channel, as the case may be;

1. Sub. by Act No. 43 of 1964, Sec. 13, for certain words (w.e.f. 27-2-1965).
2. Ins. by Act No. 43 of 1964, Sec. 13, for "The Delhi Improvement Trust" (w.e.f. 27-2-1965).

(b) to examine works under construction in the slum area to take levels or to remove, test, examine, replace or read any meter

(2) If, on such inspection, the opening of the ground is found to be necessary for the prevention of removal of a nuisance, the expenses thereby incurred shall be paid by the owner or occupier of the land or building, but if it is found that no nuisance exists or but for such opening would have arisen, the ground or portion or any building, drain, or other work opened, injured or removed for the purpose of such inspection shall be filled in, reinstated, or made good, as the case may be, by the competent authority.

24. Power to enter land adjoining land where work is in progress.—(1) Any person authorised by the competent authority in this behalf may with or without assistants or workmen, enter on any land within fifty yards of any work authorised by or under this Act for the purpose of depositing thereon any soil, gravel, stone or other materials, or for obtaining access to such work or for any other purposes connected with the carrying of the same.

(2) The person so authorised shall, before entering on any land under sub-section (1), state the purpose thereof, and shall, if so required by the occupier, or owner, fence off so much of the land as may be required for such purpose.

(3) The person so authorised, shall, in exercising any power conferred by this section, do as little damage, as may be, and compensation shall be payable by the competent authority to the owner or occupier of such land or to both for any such damage whether permanent or temporary.

25. Breaking into buildings.—It shall be lawful for any person authorised by the competent authority in this behalf to make any entry into any place, to open or cause to be opened any door, gate or other barrier—

(a) if he considers the opening thereof necessary for the purpose of such entry; and

(b) if the owner of occupier is absent, or being present refuses to open such door, gate or barrier.

26. Entry to be made in the day time.—No entry authorised by or under this Act shall be made except between the hours of sunrise and sunset.

27. Owner's consent ordinarily to be obtained.—[1][Save as provided in this Act, no building or land] shall be entered without the consent of the occupier, or if there is no occupier, of the owner thereof and no such entry shall be made without giving the said occupier or owner, as the case may be, not less than twenty-four hours' written notice of the intention of make such entry:

Provided that no such notice shall be necessary if the place to be inspected is a shed for cattle or a latrine, urinal or a work under construction.

28. Power of eviction to be exercised only by the competent authority.—Where the competent authority is satisfied either upon a representation from the owner of a building or upon other information in its possession that the occupants of the building have not vacated it in pursuance of any notice, order or direction issued or given by the authority, the authority shall, by order, direct the eviction of the occupants from the building in such manner and within such time as may be specified in the order [2][and for the purpose of such eviction may use or cause to be used such force as may be necessary]:

Provided that before making any order under this section the competent authority shall give a reasonable opportunity to the occupants of the building to show cause why they should not be evicted therefrom.

29. Power to remove offensive or dangerous trades from slum areas.—The Competent Authority may, by order in writing, direct any person carrying on any dangerous or offensive trade in a slum area to remove the trade from that area within such time as may be specified in the order:

Provided that no order under this section shall be made unless the person carrying on the trade has been afforded a reasonable opportunity of showing cause as to why the order should not be made.

30. Appeals.—(1) Except as otherwise expressly provided in this Act, any person aggrieved by any notice, order or direction issued or given by the competent authority may appeal

1. Sub. by Act No. 43 of 1964, Sec. 14, for "No building or land" (w.e.f. 27-2-1965).
2. Ins. by Act No. 43 of 1964, Sec. 15, (w.e.f. 27-2-1965).

to the Administrator within a period of thirty days from the date of issue of such notice, order or direction.

(2) Every appeal under this Act shall be made by petition in writing accompanied by a copy of the notice, order or direction appealed against.

(3) On the admission of an appeal, all proceedings to enforce the notice, order or direction and all prosecutions for any contravention thereof shall be held in abeyance pending the decision of the appeal, and if the notice, order or direction is set aside on appeal, disobedience thereto shall not be deemed to be an offence.

(4) No appeal shall be decided under this section unless the appellate has been heard or has had a reasonable opportunity of being heard in person or through a legal practitioner.

(5) The decision of the Administrator on appeal shall be final and shall not be questioned in any court.

31. Service of notices, etc.—(1) Every notice, order or direction issued under this Act shall, save as otherwise expressly provided in this Act, be served—

(a) by giving or tendering the notice, order or direction, or by sending it by post to the person for whom it is intended; or

(b) if such person cannot be found, by affixing the notice, order or direction on some conspicuous part of his last known place of abode or business, or by giving or tendering the notice, order or direction to some adult male member or servant of his family or by causing it to be affixed on some conspicuous part of the building or land, if any, to which it relates.

(2) Where the person on whom a notice, order or direction is to be served is a minor, service upon his guardian or upon any adult male member or servant of his family shall be deemed to be the service upon the minor.

(3) Every notice, order or direction which by or under this Act is to be served as a public notice, order or direction or as a notice, order or direction which is not required to be served to any individual therein specified shall, save as otherwise expressly provided, be deemed to be sufficiently served if a copy thereof is affixed in such conspicuous part of the office of the competent authority or in such other public place during

such period, or is published in such local newspaper or in such other manner, as the competent authority may direct.

32. Penalties.—(1) Whoever [1][fails to comply with] any notice, order or direction issued or given under this Act shall be punishable with imprisonment for a term which may extend to three months, or with fine which may extend to one thousand rupees, or with both.

(2) Whoever commences or causes to be commenced any work in contravention of any restriction or condition imposed under sub-section (7) of section 10 or any plan for the re-development of a clearance area shall be punishable with imprisonment which may extend a three months, or with fine which may extend to one thousand rupees, or with both.

(3) Whoever obstructs the entry of any person authorised under this Act to enter into or upon any building or land or molests such person after such entry shall be punishable with fine which may extend to one thousand rupees.

(4) If the person committing an offence under this Act is a company, every person who at the time the offence was committed was in charge of, and was responsible to, the company for the conduct of the business of the company as well as the company, shall be deemed to be guilty of the offence and shall be liable to be proceeded against and punished accordingly:

Provided that nothing contained in this sub-section shall render any such person liable to any punishment provided in this Act if he proves that the offence was committed without his knowledge or that he exercised all due diligence to prevent the commission of such offence.

(5) Notwithstanding anything contained in sub-section (3) where an offence under this Act has been committed by a company and it is proved that the offence has been committed with the consent or connivance of, or is attributable to any neglect on the part of, any director, manager, secretary or other officer of the company, such director, manager, secretary or other officer shall also be deemed to be guilty of that offence and shall be liable to be proceeded against and punished accordingly.

---

1. Sub. by Act No. 43 of 1964, Sec. 16, for "does any act in contravention of" (w.e.f. 27-2-1965).

Explanation.—For the purposes of this section—

(a) "company" means a body corporate and includes a firm or other association of individuals; and

(b) "director" in relation to a firm means a partner in the firm.

33. Order of demolition of buildings in certain cases.— [1][(1)] Where the erection of any building has been commenced, or is being carried out or has been completed, in contravention of any restriction or condition imposed under sub-section (7) of section 10 or a plan for the redevelopment of any clearance area or in contravention of any notice, order or direction issued or given under this Act the competent authority may, in addition to any other remedy that may be resorted to under this Act or under any other law, make an order directing that such erection shall be demolished by the owner thereof within such time not exceeding two months as may be specified in the order, and on the failure of the owner to comply with the order, the competent authority may itself cause the erection to be demolished and the expenses of such demolition shall be recoverable from the owner as arrears of land revenue:

Provided that no such order shall be made unless the owner has been given a reasonable opportunity of being heard.

[2][(2) For the purpose of causing any building to be demolished under sub-section (1), the competent authority may use or cause to be used such force as may be necessary.]

34. Jurisdiction of courts.—No court inferior to that of a magistrate of the first class shall try an offence punishable under his Act.

35. Previous sanction of the competent authority or officer authorised by it for prosecution.—No prosecution for any offence punishable under this Act shall be instituted except with the previous sanction of the competent authority or an officer authorised by the competent authority in this behalf.

36. Power to delegate.—[3][(1) The competent authority may, by notification in the Official Gazette, direct that any power

---

1. Section 33 re-numbered as sub-section (1) of that section by Act No. 43 of 1964, Sec. 17, (w.e.f. 27-2-1965).
2. Ins. by Act No. 43 of 1964, Sec. 17, (w.e.f. 27-2-1965).
3. Section 36 re-numbered as sub-section (1) of that section by Act No. 43 of 1964, Sec. 18 (w.e.f. 27-2-1965).

exercisable by it under this Act may also be exercised, in such cases and subject to such conditions, if any, as may be specified in the notification, by such officer or the local authority as may be mentioned therein.

[1][(2) The Central Government may, by notification in the Official Gazette, direct that any power exercisable by the Administrator under sub-section (7) of section 10, section 15, section 20 and section 30 may, subject to such conditions, if any, as may be specified in the notification, be exercised also by the Chief Secretary or by such other officer as may be mentioned therein.]

37. Protection of action taken in good faith.—No suit prosecution or other legal proceeding shall lie against the competent authority or against any person for anything which is in good faith done or intended to be done under this Act or the rules made thereunder.

[2][**37A. Bar of jurisdiction.**—Save as otherwise expressly provided in this Act, no civil court shall have jurisdiction in respect of any matter which the competent authority or any other person is empowered by or under this Act, to determine and no injunction shall be granted by any court or other authority in respect of any action taken or to be taken in pursuance of any power conferred by or under this Act.]

38. Competent authority, etc., to be public servants.—The competent authority and any person authorised by [3][it] under this Act shall be deemed to be public servants within the meaning of section 21 of the Indian Penal Code (45 of 1860).

39. Act to override other laws.—The provisions of this Act and the rules made thereunder shall have effect notwithstanding anything inconsistent therewith contained in any other law.

40. Power to make rules.—(1) The Central Government may, by notification in the Official Gazette, make rules to carry out the purposes of this Act.

---

1. Ins. by Act No. 43 of 1964, Sec. 18 (w.e.f. 27-2-1965).
2. Ins. by Act No. 43 of 1964, Sec. 19 (w.e.f. 27-2-1965).
3. Sub. by Act No. 58 of 1960, Sec. 3 and Sch. II, for "him".

(2) In particular and without prejudice to the generality of the foregoing power such rules may provide for all or any of the following matters, namely:—

(a) the manner of authentication of notices, orders and other instruments of the competent authority;

(b) the preparation of plans for the re-development of any slum area, and matters to be included in such plans;

[1][(bb) the form in which an application under sub-section (3) of section 6A shall be made and the information to be furnished and the fees to be levied in respect of such application;

(bbb) the manner in which inquiries may be held under sections 15 and 19;]

(c) the form and manner in which applications for permission under sub-section (2) of section 19 shall be made and the fees to be levied in respect of such applications;

(d) the procedure to be followed [1][and the factors to be taken into consideration] by the competent authority before granting or refusing to grant permission under section 19;

(e) the time within which an appeal may be preferred under [2][sub-section (7) of section 10 or section 20];

[1][(ee) the time within which a declaration may be filed under sub-section (1) or an intimation may be sent under sub-section (4) of section 20A and the fees, if any, to be levied in respect of such declaration;

(eee) the time within which plans, estimates and other particulars referred to in sub-section (2) of section 20A may be furnished.

(eeee) the procedure to be followed by the competent authority for fixing the provisional rent under sub-section (2) of section 20A;

(eeeee) the manner in which the rent provisionally determined under section 20A shall be communicated to the tenants and owners;

---

1. Ins. by Act No. 43 of 1964, Sec. 20 (w.e.f. 27-2-1965).
2. Subs. by Act No. 43 of 1964, Sec. 20 for "section 20" (w.e.f. 27-2-1965).

(eeecce) the matters in respect of which provision may be made under sub-section (5) of section 20B;]

(f) the officers and local authorities to whom powers may be delegated under section 36; and

(g) any other matter which has to be, or may be, prescribed.

[1][(3) Every rule made under this section shall be laid as soon as may be after it is made before each House of Parliament while it is in session for a total period of thirty days which may be comprised in one session or [2][in two or more successive sessions, and if, before the expiry of the session immediately following the session, or the successive sessions aforesaid] both Houses agree in making any modification in the rule or both Houses agree that the rule should not be made, the rate shall thereunder have effect only in such modified form or be of no effect, as the case may be; so however that any such modification or annulment shall be without prejudice to the validity of anything previously done under that rule.

THE SCHEDULE

(*See* section 15)

PRINCIPLES FOR DETERMINATION OF THE NET AVERAGE MONTHLY INCOME

1. The competent authority shall first determine the gross rent actually derived by the owner of the land acquired including any building on such land during the period of five consecutive years referred to in sub-section (1) of section 15.

(2) For such determination the competent authority may hold any local inquiry and obtain, if necessary, certified copies of extracts from the property tax assessment books of the municipal or other local authority concerned showing the rental value of such land.

3. The net average monthly income referred to in sub-section (1) of section 15 shall be sixty per cent of the average monthly gross rent which shall be one-sixtieth of the gross rent during the five consecutive years as determined by the competent authority under paragraph 1.

---

1. Subs. by Act No. 43 of 1964, Sec. 20 for sub-section (3) (w.e.f. 27-2-1965).
2. Subs. by Act No. 4 of 1986, Sec 2 and Sch., for certain words (w.e.f. 15-5-1986).

4. Forty per cent of the gross monthly rental referred to above shall not be taken into consideration in determining the net average monthly income but shall be deducted in lieu of the expenditure which the owner of the land would normally incur for payment of any property tax to the municipal or other local authority, for collection charges, income-tax or bad debts as well as for works of repair and maintenance of the buildings, if any, on the land.

5. Where the land or any portion thereof has been unoccupied or the owner has not been in receipt of any rent for the occupation of the land during the whole or any part of the said period of five years, the gross rent shall be taken to be the income which the owner would in fact have derived if the land had been leased out for rent during the said period, and for this purpose the rent actually derived from the land during a period prior or subsequent to the period during which it remained vacant or from similar land in the vicinity shall be taken into account.

Sources

1. Govt. of India, Ministry of Law, Justice and Company Affairs, The Slum Areas (Improvement and Clearance) Act, 1956 (96 of 1956).
   (As modified upto the 1st October, 1981)
2. Sehgal, Sangita Dhingra
   An Exhaustive Guide to The Slum Area (Improvement and Clearance) Act, 1956
   The Slum Areas (Improvement and Clearance) Rules, 1957. Universal Law Pvblishing Co. Pvt. Ltd. 1998. Pages 127.

ANNEXURE III

THE SLUM AREAS (IMPROVEMENT AND CLEARANCE) RULES, 1957[1]

In exercise of the powers conferred by section 40 of the Slum Areas (Improvement and Clearance) Act, 1956 (96 of 1956), the Central Government hereby makes the following rules, namely:—

1. Short title—These rules may be called the Slum Areas (Improvement and Clearance) Rules, 1957.

2. Definitions.—In these rules—

(a) "Act" means the Slum Area (Improvement and Clearance) Act, 1956 (96 of 1956).

(b) "Form" means a Form appended to these rules.

3. Forms of Notices.—Notices issued under the Act shall be in the appropriate Form appended to these rules.

4. Authentication of Notices.—Every notice issued by the competent authority under the Act shall be signed either by the competent authority or an officer authorised in this behalf by the competent authority and notices shall be deemed to be properly signed if it bears a facsimile of the signature of that authority or officer.

5. Authentication of order and other instruments.—Every notice issued by the competent authority under the Act shall be signed either by the competent authority or an officer authorised in this behalf by the competent authority and notices shall be deemed to be properly signed if it bears a facsimile of the signature of that authority of officer.

6. Plan for re-development.—Every plan for the re-development of any slum area shall include the following, namely:—

(a) description of the properties proposed for acquisition;

(b) description of the properties which may fit in the re-development plan either in their present form or after carrying out certain additions, alterations or

1. *Vide* S.R.O. 4882, published in the Gazette of India, 1957, Part II, Sec. 3., p. 294.

improvement; the latter case the additions, alterations or improvements to be made;

(c) roads, open spaces and site or sites for schools, hospitals, shopping centres, maternity and child welfare centres and similar amenities;

[1][**6A. Form of application under section 6A and fees therefor.**—(1) An application under sub-section (3) of section 6A of the Act shall be made in Form AA.

(2) The fees to be levied in respect of every such application shall be Rs. 10].

[2][**7. Form of application under section 19 and fees therefor.**—(1) An application under sub-section (2) of section 19 of the Act shall—

(i) where such application relates to the grant of permission to institute a suit or proceeding for the eviction of a tenant, be made in Form CC, and

(ii) where such application relates to the grant of permission to execute a decree or order of eviction of a tenant, be made in Form CCC.

(2) The fees to be levied in respect of every such application shall be Rs. 10.

(3) Every such application shall be accompanied by copies of relevant documents and in the case of an application for grant of permission to execute a decree or order of eviction of a tenant, also by a copy of the decree or order.

7A. Procedure to be followed by the competent authority.—(1) On receipt of an application under rule 7, the competent authority shall, for the purpose of giving an opportunity to the parties of being heard, fix a date for hearing the parties and cause a notice (intimating such date) to be issued to them.

(2) On the date fixed for hearing, or on such other date or dates to which the hearing may be adjourned, the competent authority shall hear the parties, examine the witnesses, if any, produced, and the documents filed, by them.

(3) If either of the parties is absent on any date of hearing,

---

1. Ins. by the Slum Areas (Improvement and Clearance) Amendment Rules, 1973, rule 2(1).
2. Sub. by the Slum Areas (Improvement and Clearance) Amendment Rules, 1973, rule 2(2) for rule 7.

the competent authority may in his absence, and after hearing the party present, pass such order, as it thinks fit.

[1][**8. Period of limitation for filing appeals.**—An appeal under sub-section (7) of section 20 of the Act shall be fixed within a period of thirty days from the date of communication of the order appealed against.

[2][**9. Time limit for filing declaration under section 20A(1) and fees therefor.**—(1) A declaration by a tenant under sub-section (1) of section 20A of the Act shall be filed within fifteen days from the date on which the tenant vacates the building or, as the case may be, on which he is evicted from the building.

(2) The fees to be levied in respect of every such declaration shall be Rs. 5.

10. Time limit within which plans, estimates and other particulars are to be furnished under sub-section (2) of section 20A.—The time limit for furnishing plans, estimates and other particulars by the owners of a building under sub-section (2) of section 20A of the Act shall be ten days than the date of the order of the competent authority under that sub-section requiring the owner to furnish the same.

11. Manner of communication of rent provisionally determined.—The rent provisionally determined under sub-section (2) of section 20A of the Act shall be communicated to the tenant and the owner in writing by registered post under acknowledgement due.

12. Time limit for intimation under sub-section (4) of section 20A.—The time limit for intimation by a tenant under sub-section (4) of section 20A of the Act shall be fifteen days from the date of receipt of the communication of the determination of provisional rent to him under sub-section (3) of that section.]

---

1. Sub. by the Slum Areas (Improvement and Clearance) Amendment Rules, 1973, rule 2(3).
2. Ins. by the Slum Areas (Improvement and Clearance) Amendment Rules, 1973, rule 2(4).

SCHEDULE

Form A

Notice under section 4(1) of the Slum Areas (Improvement and Clearance) Act, 1956

To

____

____

Whereas I, ..., the Competent Authority, am satisfied upon report from ..../ other information in my possession, that the building(s) *................. in **...................... declared to be a 'Slum Area' under section 3(1) of the Slum Areas (Improvement and Clearance) Act, 1956, is/are for human habitation in the following respects:—

(1)
(2)
(3)
(4)

Now, therefore, in pursuance of the powers conferred upon me under section 4(1) of the said Act, I hereby require you, owner(s) of the building to execute the works of improvement mentioned in the Schedule below within 30 days of the receipt of this notice, as in my opinion these works will render the building(s) fit for human habitation.

In case you fail to comply with this notice, I shall get these works executed under section 5 of the Act and all expenses so incurred together with interest at the rate of six per cent per annum from the date of demand shall be recovered from you as arrears of land revenue.

Competent Authority

* Specify the building(s)
**Specify the area.

Note.—The items not required should be struck out.

[1][**FORM AA**

[Rule 6A(1)]

Application for the grant of permission to erect building in slum areas

To

The Competent Authority,
Slum Areas,
Delhi

Dear Sir,

I/We am/are the owner(s) of the building bearing Municipal No. (s) .... Ward No.................................. situated at ....

2. It is requested that permission be granted under sub-section (1) of section 6A of the Slum Areas (Improvement and Clearance) Act, 1956 for the erection of the said building.

3. The prescribed fee of Rs. 10 has been paid *vide* cash receipt No. .... date the ....

4. The details of the proposed erection are given below:

(a) ....

(b) ....

(c) ....

(d) ....

(e) ....

(d) ....

(f) ....

(g) ....

Yours faithfully,
Signature(s) of the applicant (s)

Present address of the applicant(s)

....

....

....

Dated: ....].

---

1. Ins. by the Slum Areas (Improvement and Clearance) Amendment Rules, 1973, rule 2(5).

FORM B

Notice under section 7(1) of the Slum Areas (Improvement and Clearance) Act, 1956

To

....

....

Whereas I, ..., the Competent Authority, am satisfied upon report from ..../ other information in my possession, that the building(s)* .... in **........................ declared to be a 'Slum Area' under section 3(1) of the Slum Areas (Improvement and Clearance) Act, 1956 is/are unfit for human habitation and is/are not capable at a reasonable expense of being rendered so fit.

Now, therefore, in pursuance of the powers conferred upon me under section 7(1) of the said Act, I hereby call upon you an owner, lesses or mortgagee, or any other person having an interest in the building(s) to show cause within 15 days of the receipt of this notice as to why an order for demolition of the building(s) should not be made.

Competent Authority

* Specify the building(s)

**Specify the area.

Note.—The items not required should be struck out.

FORM C

Notice under the provision to section 12(1) of the Slum Areas (Improvement and Clearance) Act, 1956

To

....

....

Whereas on representation from the Competent Authority under the Slum Areas (Improvement and Clearance) Act, 1956, it appears to the Central Government that in order to enable to the authority to execute work(s) of improvement in relation to* .... in** .... declared to be a Slum Area to re-develop .... declared to be a Clearance Area, it is necessary that the land(s) specified in the schedule below and adjoining/surrounded by such area should be acquired. You

.... as owner/any other person interested in the said land(s) are hereby called upon to show cause within 15 days of the receipt of this notice as to why it should not be acquired.

You may address your objections, if any, to the Secretary to the Government of India, Ministry of Health, New Delhi.

Dy Secretary to the Govt. of India.

* Specify the buildings(s).

**Specify the area.

[1][FORM CC

[Rule 7(1)(i)]

Application under section 19 of the Slum Areas (Improvement and Clearance) Act, 1956 for permission to institute a suit or proceeding for eviction of a tenant

To

The Competent Authority,
Slum Areas,
Delhi

Dear Sir,

I/We am/are the owner(s) of the premises bearing Municipal No. (s) ....

2. .... is/are tenant(s) in the said premises with effect from ....

3. It is requested that permission be granted under clause (a) of sub-section (1) of section 19 of the Slum Areas (Improvement and Clearance) Act, 1956 permitting the owner(s) of the said premises to institute a suit or proceeding for obtaining a decree or order for the eviction of the aforesaid tenant(s) from ....

4. The ground on which eviction of the tenant is sought are:

(a) ....

(b) ....

(c) ....

(d) ....

5. The prescribed fee of Rs. 10 has been paid *vide* cash receipt No. .... dated ....

1. Ins. by the Slum Areas (Improvement and Clearance) Amendment Rules, 1973, rule 2(6).

6. The various addresses of the tenant(s) are given below:

(a) ....

(b) ....

(c) ....

(d) ....

Yours faithfully,
Signature(s) of the applicant(s)

Address

....

....

Dated ....]

FORM CCC

[Rule 7(1)(ii)]

Application under section 19 of the Slum Areas (Improvement and Clearance) Act, 1956, for permission to evict a tenant under a decree or order

To

The Competent Authority,
Slum Areas,
Delhi

Dear Sir,

I/We having obtained a decree or order for the eviction .... from .... hereby apply for permission to execute such decree or order.

2. Copies of decree or order and judgement (if any) are enclosed.

3. The prescribed fee of Rs. 10 has been paid *vide* receipt No.(s) .... dated ....

4. The special grounds on which this permission is sought are:

(i) ....

(ii) ....

Yours faithfully,
Signatures of applicant(s).]

FORM D

Notice under section 27 of the Slum Areas (Improvement and Clearance) Act, 1956

To

....

....

You are hereby given notice under section 27 of the Slum Areas (Improvement and Clearance) Act, 1956, that I, ..., being duly authorised in this behalf by the Competent Authority, propose to enter with/without assistants and workmen, the building/land .... under your occupation/ ownership at .... on .... for the purpose of ....

Signature of Officer

FORM E

Notice under section 29 of the Slum Areas (Improvement and Clearance) Act, 1956

To

....

....

Whereas you are carrying on the trade of ...., a dangerous or offensive trade in *.................... an area declared to be 'Slum Area' under section 3(1) of the Slum Areas (Improvement and Clearance) Act, 1956, I, ..., the Competent Authority, hereby call upon you under section 29 of the said Act to show cause within 15 days of the receipt of this notice as to why an order directing you to remove the said trade from the said area should not be made.

Competent Authority

* Specify the area

FORM F

Notice under section 33 of the Slum Areas (Improvement and Clearance) Act, 1956

To

....

....

Whereas you have commenced/and carrying out/have completed the erection of a building consisting of .... in contravention of ....

The restrictions/conditions imposed under section 10(7) of the Slum Areas (Improvement and Clearance) Act, 1956 or the plan for the development of any clearance area or the notice/ order/direction issue under given the said Act.

You are hereby informed that you may appear before the undersigned at .... on .... in this office and make your objection or representation, if any.

Competent Authority

Note.—The items not required should be struck down.

Select Bibliography

Books

Aldrich, B.C. and Sandu, R.S. (1995). "The Global context of housing poverty", *Housing the Urban Poor-Policy and Practice in Developing countries,* Aldrich B.S. and Ranshu R.S. (eds), Vistar Publications, New Delhi, pp.17–33.

Birdi, H.D. (1982). *Delhi-Slum and Law: A Comparative Study of India and Foreign Law*, I.S.S.D., New Delhi.

Bose, A. (1993). *Studies in India's Urbanization, 1901–1971*, Tata McGraw Hill Publishing Co. Ltd., Bombay.

De Souza, S. (1983). *The Indian City: Poverty, Ecology and Urban Development*, Manohar Publications, New Delhi.

Desai, A.R. and Pillai S.D. (eds), (1970). *Slums and Urbanization*, Popular Prakashan, Bombay.

Dhadave, M.S. (1989). *Sociology of Slum*, Archives Books, New Delhi.

Hardoy, J.E. and Satterthwaite, D. (1989). *Squatter Citizen: Life in the Urban Third World*, Earthscan Publications Ltd., London.

Iyar, V.R.K. (1988). *Land and Urban Poor in India*, B.R. Publishing Corporation, Delhi.

Kundu, A. (1993). *In the Name of Urban Poor: Access to Basic Amenities*, Sage Publications, New Delhi.

Lahiri, T.B. (1978). "Calcutta—A Million City with a Million Problems", *Million Cities of India,* Mishra, R.P. (ed.), Vikas Publishing House, New Delhi, pp. 48–56.

Majumdar, T.K. (1978). "The Urban Poor and Social Change: A Study of Squatter Settlement in Delhi", *The Indian City Poverty, Ecology and Urban Development*, Manohar Publications, pp. 29–60.

Mehra, A.K. (1991). *The Politics of Urban Redevelopment: A Study at Old Delhi*, Sage Publications, New Delhi.

Nangia, Sudesh (1989). 'Integration of Urban Poor in Physical and Social Development Planning in Megacities of Developing Regions' Published in *Population Transition in India,* S.N. Singh, M.K. Premi, P.S. Bhatia, Ashish Bose (eds).

Premi, M.K., Ramanamma, A. and Bambawala, U. (n.d.) *An Introduction to Social Demography*, Vikas Publishing House, New Delhi.

Ramachandran, R. (1989). *Urbanization, Occupational Mobility and Social Integration: A Study of S.C.*

Rao, K.R. and Rao, M.S.A. (1984). Cities and Slums—A Study of a Squatter's Settlement in the City of Vijayawada, Concept Publishing Company, New Delhi.

Singh, A.M. and De Souza, A. (eds) (1989). The Urban Poor—Slum and Pavement Dwellers in the Metropolitan Cities of India, Manhar Publications, New Delhi.

Singh, H.H. and Kumar, K.K. (eds), (1985). "Slums: Threat to Urban Environment" *Geography and Environment Issues and Challenges,* Concept Publishing Company, New Delhi, pp. 113–37.

Singh, K. and Steinberg, F. (eds) (1996). *Urban India in the Cities of Bihar:* with special reference to Patna, Patna Improvement Trust, Patna.

Sur, P. (1994). *Urban Poor: Their Housing Needs and Government Response,* Har-Anand Publcations, New Delhi.

Venkatarayappa, N.K. (1992). *Slums: A Study in Urban Problems,* Sterling Publishers Pvt., Ltd., New Delhi.

Articles

Ali, S. (1989). "A Low Cost Sanitation Scheme for Slum Dwellers of Delhi", *Social Change*, vol. 19, no. 4, December, pp. 93–102.

Ali, S. (1992). "Garbage Problems in Two Resettlement Colonies in Delhi", *Social Change*, vol. 22, no. 1, March, pp. 93–102.

Khatu, B.N. (1975). "Baroda Slums: A Case Study in Misuse of Land", Deccan Geography, No. 13, pp. 225–34.

Kundu, A. (1991). "Micro Environment in Urban Planning—Access of the Poor to the Water Supply and Sanitation", *Economic and Political Weekly* vol. 26, no. 37, pp. 2167–71.

Nangia, Sudesh (1988). "Slums of Urban India", *Asian Urbanization Problems and Prospects,* Frank J. Costa, Ashok K. Dutt, Laurence, J.C, and Allen G. Noble (eds), Chapter 12, pp. 131–42. (Published by Gebrider Bornlraeger, Berlin).

Premi, M.K. (1984). "Internal Migration in India 1961–81" *Social Actioin*, vol. 34, July–September, pp. 274–85.

Rebeiro, E.F.N. (1988). "Planning for the Urban Poor: Basic Needs on Priorities", *Civic Affairs,* vol. 35, no. 8, March, pp. 23–32.

Roy, P. and others (1992). "Measuring Bustee Environment in Calcutta", *Social Change,* vol. 22, no. 1, March, pp. 120–39.

Sahani, R.A. (1980). "Slums: The Backlash of Rural Poverty, Bombay's Slum World", *Social Welfare* vol. 27, no. 1–2, pp, 9–11.

Seth, H.K. (1987). "How to Prevent Future Growth of Slums", *Mainstream*, vol. 25, no. 29, April, pp. 28–30.

Shafi, S.S. (1995). "India's Urban Crisis", *Patriot,* 16 January.

Sidharan, N. and Razak, A.M. (1994). "Linkage and Planning

Process—Issues in Informal Settlement Planning" Indian Town Planning Institute', vol. 12, no. 3, pp. 31–43.
Singh, S.N. and Yadav, K.N.S. (1974). "A Study of Pattern of Rural Urban Migration", *Demography India*, vol. 3, no. 2, pp. 278–86.
Swamy, M.C.K. (1987). "Slums: Ruralization of Urban India", *Nagarlok*, vol. 19, no. 2, pp. 22–28.
Yeshwanth, I. (1980). "Life of Slums in Madras", *Social Welfare*, vol. 27, no. 1–2.

Reports and other Documents

Bharat Sevak Samaj (1958). Slums of Old Delhi, Report of the Socio-Economic Survey of the Slum Dwellers of Old Delhi, Atma Ram and Sons, New Delhi.
Census of India (1981). General Economic Tables Part III-A(i), Registrar General of India, pp. 31–44.
Economic Conditions of Slum Dwellers, National Sample Survey, 31st Round (July 1976–July 1977).
Gill, H.S. (1994). *Housing the Poor: An Analysis with Special Reference to Slum Colonies in Delhi*, Unpublished Ph.D. thesis, CSRD, JNU.
Institute of Town Planners, India (1982). Delhi: Past, Present and Future, Souvenir, New Delhi.
Nangia, P. and Gupta K. (1993). "Morphology of Slums in Thane", IIPS Research Report Series 1993–94, no. 6 IIPS Bombay, pp. 1–61.
NSSO 31st Round (1976–77) Survey on Socio-Economic Conditions of Households in Slums in Metropolitan Cities Report 301/1–7, 1993.
Pathak, C.R. (1983). *Environment Problems of Calcutta, City*, ISEMA Abstract, NATMO, Calcutta, 1993.
Press Clippers
Kundu, A., Policy Perspective on Urban Land and Housing, *Patriot* (New Delhi), 18th May 1988.
Matheu, T., Economic Aspects of Housing, *Financial Express*, 30th December 1987.
Qazi, M. Rootless Millions Multiply, Deccan Herald, 11th November 1989.
Sachar, R. Time to Ensure Housing Rights to All, *Hindustan Times*, 6th July 1996.
Shafi, S.S. India's Urban Crisis, *Patriot*, 16th January 1995.
Shourie, H.D. Frightening Facts on Housing, *The Statesman*, 16th January 1988.
Wig, A.R. Sensible Housing Policy at Last, *Hindustan Times*, 24th January 1988.

Index